Men-at-Arms • 555

The Union Army 1861–65 (2)

Eastern and New England States

Ron Field • Illustrated by Marco Capparoni

Series editors Martin Windrow & Nick Reynolds

OSPREY PUBLISHING

Bloomsbury Publishing Plc

Kemp House, Chawley Park, Cumnor Hill, Oxford OX2 9PH, UK

29 Earlsfort Terrace, Dublin 2, Ireland

1385 Broadway, 5th Floor, New York, NY 10018, USA

E-mail: info@ospreypublishing.com

www.ospreypublishing.com

OSPREY is a trademark of Osprey Publishing Ltd

First published in Great Britain in 2024

A catalog record for this book is available from the British Library.

ISBN: PB 9781472855831; eBook 9781472855800;
ePDF 9781472855824; XML 9781472855817

24 25 26 27 28   10 9 8 7 6 5 4 3 2 1

Index by Rob Munro

Typeset by PDQ Digital Media Solutions, Bungay, UK

Printed and bound in India by Replika Press Private Ltd.

MIX
Paper from responsible sources
FSC® C016779
FSC   www.fsc.org

Osprey Publishing supports the Woodland Trust, the UK's leading woodland conservation charity.

To find out more about our authors and books visit **www.ospreypublishing. com**. Here you will find extracts, author interviews, details of forthcoming events and the option to sign up for our newsletter.

Acknowledgments

The author is grateful to the following for their help in the production of this volume: Tom, Jason, Brandon, and Christian Liljenquist for access to their collection at the Library of Congress, Washington, DC; Kay Peterson, Archives Center, Smithsonian National Museum of American History, Washington, DC; Chelsea Vasquez, Collections Assistant, Rochester Museum & Science Center, Rochester, New York; Don Troiani; Kelly Ford; Daniel J. Binder; Daniel J. Miller; Dr. Michael R. Cunningham; and Robert Grandchamp.

Title-page illustration: This lithograph from a sheet-music cover shows the officers and NCOs of the Gymnast Zouaves of Pennsylvania. Organized and trained by Louis Hildebrand at his Gymnasium during April 1861, this company expanded into a battalion by July of that year, and entered Federal service as part of the 23d Pennsylvania Volunteer Infantry (Birney's Zouaves). The NCOs wear the uniform adopted by July 1861, while the officers wear red chasseur-pattern caps with their dark-blue coats and pants. (Anne S.K. Brown Military Collection, Brown University)

THE UNION ARMY 1861–65 (2)

EASTERN AND NEW ENGLAND STATES

INTRODUCTION

The Eastern States provided about 1¼ million men for the Union cause during the Civil War. Taking up arms in the wake of the three-month volunteers who had responded to President Abraham Lincoln's call on April 15, 1861, these men joined the ranks during 1861–65 for two or three years, six or nine months, or 100 days. They were supplemented by thousands of draftees, plus various militia organizations. Initially, many wore gray uniforms, which led to confusion with Confederates on the battlefield and casualties from friendly fire, particularly at the battles of Big Bethel (June 10, 1861) and First Bull Run (July 21, 1861).

It was not until August 1861 that the Union Army took the first steps to standardize blue as the color of uniform for its troops. On August 21, Major General George B. McClellan, commanding the Military Division of the Potomac, issued orders forbidding the purchase of gray uniforms. Four days later, McClellan wrote to Secretary of War Simon Cameron suggesting that no more Union troops "be uniformed in gray" (ORs 1899: 453). On September 23, 1861, Assistant Secretary of War Thomas A. Scott issued a War Department Circular to State Governors stating: "The Department respectfully requests that no troops hereafter furnished by your State for the service of the Government be uniformed in gray, that being the color generally worn by the enemy. The blue uniform adopted for the Army of the United States is recommended as readily distinguishable from that of the enemy" (ORs 1899: 531). During November of that year, Quartermaster General Montgomery C. Meigs invited proposals from contractors to provide uniforms for much of the Union Army, stating: "Light or dark blue cloths preferred, and light grays will not be considered" (*NAUSG*, November 13, 1861: 2.3).

By the end of 1861 most Union troops were expected to be clothed in regulation-pattern blue Army uniforms consisting of a nine-button Pattern 1854 frock coat with sky-blue or scarlet trim, sky-blue trousers, and black felt Pattern 1858 hat, or a four-button sack coat and forage cap. Cavalry and light artillery wore mounted service jackets with yellow or scarlet trim respectively. Nevertheless, some Eastern states clothed their troops in state-pattern uniforms while many fielded units wearing colorful Zouave or chasseur uniforms. Even when the War Department revoked the right of states to clothe their regiments prior to muster into Federal service on March 31, 1864, some state-pattern uniforms previously made and issued continued to be worn.

This unidentified New York private wears an example of the brownish-gray uniform issued to many New York regiments in 1861 due to a shortage of blue cloth. The state-pattern jacket has an eight-button front, shoulder straps, and three small buttons on each cuff flap. A gray chasseur-pattern cap with dark band rests on his knee. (Author's collection)

The jacket worn by Sergeant William Brownell of the Rochester Light Guard (Co. A), 13th New York Infantry, is based on the pattern established by the New York Military Board in April 1861. Note the welt, or slit, pocket low on the right breast. A small oiled-cloth pouch hangs from the lowest button. (Courtesy of the RMSC, Rochester, NY)

The surviving jacket of Sergeant Rollin B. Truesdell (27th New York Volunteer Infantry) is an example of the pattern issued to New York volunteers from June 1861. (Military & Historical Image Bank Cwu69ds)

NEW YORK

The most populous and wealthiest state in the Union, New York provided 400,680 soldiers during the Civil War. Of this number, 46,534 died in battle or from wounds or disease (Eicher & Eicher 2001: 54 & 62). These men were organized into 248 regiments and seven companies of infantry; 27 regiments of cavalry and mounted rifles plus ten independent cavalry companies; 15 artillery regiments and 35 light batteries; and four regiments of engineers (Phisterer 1883: 14).

On April 16, 1861, the New York State Legislature passed a bill providing for the enrollment of 30,000 troops to take the place of the three-month volunteer militia and to serve for two years. As a result, Governor Edwin D. Morgan ordered the establishment of 38 new regiments numbered in a new series commencing with the "1st," and whose designation was changed from "militia" to "volunteers."

The authorization of these new regiments presented the state with major clothing problems. Being informed that the Federal government would attempt to equip but could not uniform these regiments, New York created a Military Board that procured clothing plus much of the equipage needed. The uniform established by the state for its troops on April 22 was described as "a jacket of dark army blue cloth, cut to flow from the waist and to fall about four inches below the belt. The coat to be buttoned with eight buttons … a low standing collar … buttons to be those of the State militia." The pants and overcoat were described as "light army blue," with the former "cut full in the leg and large around the foot." The overcoat was to be "of the pattern worn by the United States infantry." Headgear consisted of "a fatigue cap of dark blue, with a water-proof cover, to be made with a cape which will fall to the shoulder. The cover to be buttoned at the visor, and furnished with strings, so that it may be tied under the chin." The state button was also used on the overcoat and cap ("Communication" 1862: 13).

On April 25, a contract was duly awarded by Military Board Treasurer Philip Dorsheimer to Brooks Brothers of New York City to supply 12,000 jackets, pairs of pants, and overcoats. Although the original cost of this uniform was estimated at $26, a bid from Brooks Brothers of $19.50 was accepted (*AEJ*, April 24, 1861: 2.4). Meanwhile, J.G. Cotrell & Son, and J.H. McDonald, Jr., both of Albany, were contracted to provide the caps at $12 a dozen. Murphy & Childs, of New York City, were contracted to provide the same at $11.40 a dozen. The contract for shoes was awarded to Woolverton & Co., of Albany, and Wood, Willard & Prentice, of Troy, both of which were to supply 6,000 pairs of "good stout cowhide Brogans, lined, at $1.25 a pair" (*AEJ*, April 24, 1861: 2.4). The above was sufficient to outfit 16 of the 17 new regiments the state planned to establish first, or all 17 regiments if under strength.

There were several significant details regarding the cut and trim of the uniform. The jacket had shoulder straps, a belt loop on the left side, and a breast pocket. Details varied, however. For example, the pocket could be on the right or left breast. Known as a welt, or slit, pocket, this feature was made by cutting the jacket front open and sewing additional pieces into it. Trim on the edges of the jacket collar, shoulder straps, and belt loop also varied widely in both size and color. Some of the trim was true welting, formed into a tube and sewn between the edges of the collar and shoulder straps. Other trim simply consisted of colored cord sewn to the edges. Some shoulder straps had solid facing color. The jacket was meant to extend 4in. below the waist, but many were made considerably shorter.

Soon after commencing production of the state uniform, Brooks Brothers discovered that the normal sources of US Army blue cloth were exhausted. This meant it was necessary to renegotiate the contract to permit the substitution of another type and/or color cloth – and much of what was available was gray, not blue. As the New York State Militia regulations of 1858 had already prescribed a gray nine-button jacket, permission was granted for its use. Of the jackets subsequently supplied by Brooks Brothers, 7,300 were made of a gray "cadet mixed satinet," which had a satin-like surface. A further 2,600 were of "dark blue kersey," which was a rough, coarse wool usually ribbed and, prior to this date, used mainly for enlisted men's trousers and overcoats. The remaining 2,100 were of a very inferior "dark blue felt." Regarding trousers, 7,200 pairs were produced using gray "cadet mixed satinet;" 2,400 were "dark blue kersey;" and 2,400 were light blue, all wool "army kersey." Of the overcoats, 4,400 were gray "cadet doeskin," which was a smooth, close-woven, woolen cloth; 4,000 were of "brown mixed" wool; 1,600 were of dark-blue "petersham" wool; and 2,000 were "mixed kersey" (Todd 1983: 1018).

Before the completion of the Brooks Brothers' order, the Military Board was advised that a portion of the clothing had been made from inferior cloth. An investigatory committee found that the gray uniforms supplied were entirely unsatisfactory having been made of low-grade yarn obtained by tearing to shreds woolen rags with some new wool added to make it look like a superior article. This produced a worthless fabric known as "shoddy." Various accounts of this cloth survive in the contemporary press. One described it as "a rusty gray satinet material composed of cotton and 'shotty' with a sprinkling of dog's hair and bristles" (*DUA*, May 27, 1861: 2.1).

In order to replace the shoddy clothing with better-quality uniforms, the New York State Quartermaster Department advertised for new contracts on May 23, 1861, which were let within several days, for 15,000

Armed with a Springfield Model 1842 rifled musket, this unidentified private of the 33d New York Infantry wears the dark-blue jacket trimmed with sky blue supplied by the state from June 1861. (US National Archives 111-B-5506)

Most of these enlisted men of the 5th New York Infantry (Duryée's Zouaves) wear uniforms supplied by Devlin, Hudson & Co., of New York City, including blue jackets with red worsted *tombeaux* (ornate loops) and trefoil trim. The man sitting on the ground at extreme left wears a jacket with different, lighter-colored trim on the chest and cuffs. These may be examples of the 209 uniforms supplied to the 5th New York Infantry by Wilhelm Seligman & Co., another New York City contractor who produced the regiment's uniforms. Two men who may be NCOs wear forage caps and have seam stripes on their breeches. (Author's collection)

Enlisting for two years on May 3, 1861, Robert B. Johnston was mustered-in as a sergeant in Co. H, 9th New York Infantry (Hawkins' Zouaves) the next day. He wears the second-pattern uniform issued to his regiment. (Library of Congress LC-DIG-ppmsca-71013)

This fez was worn by Sergeant Latham A. Fish, Co. K, 9th New York Infantry. (Military & Historical Image Bank CWc27ds)

blue state uniforms "to be made of the regular army standard weight ... of cloth of pure fleece wool and indigo dye ... overcoats and pantaloons of [sky blue] and jackets of a deep blue color" (Communication 1862: 120). This brought the total number of enlisted men outfitted by New York to 28,000, which included all of the first 38 volunteer regiments, plus several of the militia regiments re-organized for Federal service. Following much competition, the firms contracted to produce 2,500 suits of clothing each were: Devlin, Hudson & Co.; Wilhelm Seligman & Co.; Arnoux & Co.; Baldwin & Co.; Charles Barnum, all of New York City; and P.P. Kellogg & Co., of Utica, in Oneida County, NY ("Communication" 1862: 120). The uniforms these firms supplied were described in the press as being "made of the best cloth, and in workmanship are far superior to the clothing made for the United States Army" (*NYH*, June 23, 1861: 5.2). The contract for fatigue caps was awarded to Murphy & Childs, of New York City (*AEJ*, May 25, 1861: 1.7).

The issuance of these uniforms began about mid-June 1861, and virtually all the infantry were in receipt of the state regulation fatigue jacket, with sky-blue trousers, while the cavalry and artillery were issued jackets and pants based on US Army regulations.

From April through July 1862, the Federal government issued clothing and equipage to New York troops upon requisition of New York Quartermaster General and future president Chester A. Arthur. On July 2, a new call for troops was made by President Lincoln under which New York's allotment was 59,705 three-year volunteers and the same number for nine months' service. On the same occasion the War Department decided to allow those states that wished to resume direct issue of uniforms to their troops prior to mustering into Federal service to do so, and New York so elected (Todd 1983: 1020). Thus, during July and August 1862, the state took over a large stock of clothing from the US Deputy Quartermaster General in New York, which included about 45,000 frock coats and over 53,000 sack coats of US Army pattern. Also received back were about 40,000 New York Pattern 1861 infantry fatigue jackets. From this date onward, New York infantry units were issued via random selection either coats or jackets with state-pattern buttons for their initial uniform.

From mid-1862 until March 31, 1864, when the War Department revoked the right of states to clothe their regiments prior to muster into Federal service, New York supplied its new regiments with their initial clothing, while replacement personnel for regiments in the field drew regulation clothing from US Army quartermasters. As a result, a typical New York regiment wore several patterns of coats and jackets.

New York also recruited and clothed numerous regiments in Zouave, semi-Zouave, and chasseur-pattern uniforms throughout the Civil War. These units did all they could to ensure the continuous issuance of their colorful uniforms once their first issue had worn out.

Wearing dark-blue jackets and trousers trimmed with red, the 9th New York Infantry, or Hawkins' Zouaves, were mustered-in on April 23 and 27, 1861, with a term of service that expired in May 1863. Some men who joined the regiment after its original recruitment retained their Zouave uniforms after being transferred to the 3d US Infantry.

When a regiment of veterans was recruited to replace the 9th New York Infantry the original Hawkins' Zouave uniform began to be issued to it,

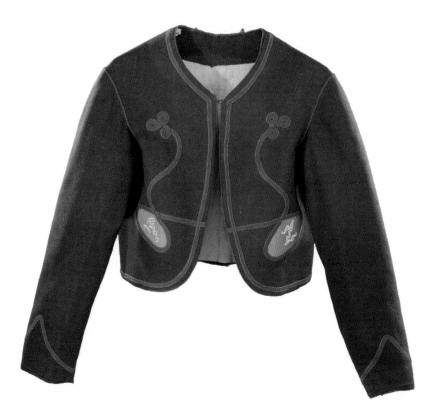

This example of the jacket worn by the 62d New York Infantry (Anderson Zouaves) has the letters "A" and "Z" embroidered in yellow thread on orange inserts in the false pockets of the *tombeaux* on the jacket front. (Smithsonian NMAH AF.64127)

but this regiment was never filled and its men were transferred to Colonel William T.C. Grower's 17th New York Veteran Infantry in October 1863. Grower was so impressed by the uniform of the 9th New York Infantry that it was adopted for his regiment and worn for the remainder of the Civil War. As a result, the Hawkins' Zouave pattern was selected by the US Quartermaster Department as a standard-pattern Zouave uniform, and was produced and issued long after the 9th New York Infantry was mustered-out. In particular, personnel of the 164th New York Infantry were issued with the Hawkins' Zouave uniform late in the war.

With the expiration of the term of service of the 5th New York Infantry on May 14, 1863, steps were taken to ensure that Zouave uniforms would still be worn within the 5th Division, V Corps, Army of the Potomac. By January 1864, three regiments of this division – the 140th and 146th New York Infantry, plus the 155th Pennsylvania Volunteer Infantry – exchanged their regular uniforms for Zouave clothing. That of the 140th New York Infantry, or "Rochester Racehorses," consisted of a dark-blue combined jacket and vest trimmed with red, dark-blue pantaloons with red trim, and a red fez with a large blue tassel, around which was worn a white turban for full dress. The uniform issued to the 146th New York Infantry, or "Garrard's Tigers," was a close copy of that worn by the *Tirailleurs algériens* (Algerian skirmishers), or Turcos, of the French Army and consisted of a light-blue jacket, vest, and pantaloons trimmed with yellow, plus a red fez with a yellow tassel.

Increased to regimental size from the Second Battalion of the 5th New York Infantry on November 29, 1862, the 165th New York Infantry, or Second Duryée Zouaves, served in the 3d Brigade, 1st Division, XIX Corps, from January 1864, and wore a uniform based on that of the

This unidentified private of Co. A, 14th Brooklyn, or 84th New York Infantry, wears a chasseur-pattern uniform. (Author's collection)

original Duryée's Zouaves, but with dark-blue fez tassel. Photographic evidence also suggests that later in the Civil War personnel of the 165th New York Infantry wore red sashes without the light-blue trim.

Volunteering for war service as the 84th New York Infantry, the 14th New York State Militia, also known as the 14th Brooklyn, wore a uniform described as consisting of "red pantaloons, blue jacket embroidered with red, and red and blue cap, similar to that of the Chasseur a Pied of France" (*NYH*, May 12, 1861: 5.2). Other chasseur-pattern uniforms were worn by the 51st, 57th, and 65th New York Volunteer Infantry, plus the Independent Battalion, New York Volunteer Infantry, or *Les Enfants Perdus* ("Lost Children"). Commanded by French Army veteran Lieutenant Colonel Felix Confort, the battalion was possibly named after a French Army unit known as *Les Enfants Perdus de Crimée* that served during the Crimean War (1853–56). Recruited in New York City during August–September 1861, enlistees for *Les Enfants Perdus* wore a full-dress uniform similar to that of the French *chasseurs à pied* (light infantry).

During August 1862 the personnel of the 73d New York Infantry, plus the 62nd, 76th, and 83d Pennsylvania Volunteer Infantry, and the 18th Massachusetts Infantry, were re-clothed in French uniforms imported by the Federal Quartermaster's Department and made by the Paris-based military outfitter Alexis Godillot, sole manufacturer of uniforms for the French Army (*NYH*, August 12, 1862: 8.1). Eager to find additional sources of clothing for his already overstretched department, Meigs placed an order on August 9, 1861, for 10,000 complete suits, plus accouterments and equipage, which were based on the Pattern 1860 *chasseurs à pied de la ligne* dress and fatigue uniforms, with the intention of eventually clothing the entire Union Army in this manner. Upon receipt, these uniforms were issued as a first step to the best-drilled regiments, as chosen by McClellan, during a review of Brigadier General Fitz-John Porter's 3d Division, III Corps, Army of the Potomac, as part of a Grand Review of the Army of the Potomac at Bailey's Crossroads, Virginia, on November 9, 1861 (*BET*, November 23, 1861: 4.1).

The full-dress uniform consisted of a dark-blue chasseur jacket with yellow braid, white metal buttons, and yellow worsted epaulets;

medium-blue pantaloons with tan leather gaiters and white leggings; black leather cap with brass plate and black cock's feather plume. Fatigue headgear consisted of a dark-blue *bonnet de police* (pointed and tasseled cap) with light-yellow piping and embroidered hunting horn at front. Also supplied were fatigue jackets, cloaks with hoods, and both leather and linen gaiters. These European uniforms proved generally too small for the average-sized American soldier, and were left with the Quartermaster's Department at Georgetown, Virginia, when McClellan finally began offensive operations on March 10, 1862.

Named after Giuseppe Garibaldi, the father of Italian unification, the 39th New York Infantry, or Garibaldi Guard, was commanded by Colonel Frederick G. D'Utassy. This multinational regiment wore a uniform based on that of the *bersaglieri* (riflemen) of Sardinia. For field officers this consisted of a dark-blue, double-breasted, chasseur-pattern coat with deep-crimson standing collar, pointed cuffs, and cord on the front and skirts, and distinctive Hungarian-style gold lace frogging across the breast. Company-grade officers and enlisted men wore a single-breasted coat faced with red trim, and narrow red stripes on the outer trouser seams. Headgear consisted of a round-topped black felt hat with black feather and eagle insignia.

First organized in November 1858, as the Highland Guard, the 79th New York State Militia was named after the 79th Regiment of Foot (Cameron Highlanders) of the British Army (*NYH*, November 10, 1858, 4:6). Adopting the Cameron of Erracht tartan, the 79th New York State Militia was described by regimental historian William Todd as wearing "handsome State jackets with red facings, blue fatigue caps and Cameron tartan pants" (Todd 1886: 5). By July 1860, the regiment had experienced great difficulty in providing its whole complement with full dress including "kilts, polka jackets, plaid stockings and bright buckled

Private Charles Hoffman, Co. A, 73d New York Infantry, wears the French uniform issued to his regiment in August 1862. (Library of Congress LC-DIG-ppmsca-72120)

FAR LEFT
Les Enfants Perdus wore a blue forage cap, coat, and pantaloons, all trimmed with yellow tape and braid. (Author's collection)

LEFT
Only Co. I of the 62d New York Infantry (Anderson Zouaves) wore full Zouave uniforms. The remainder of the regiment wore light-blue trousers with Zouave jackets, vests, and fezzes. Private Isaac Cooper of Co. A wears the latter uniform. (Library of Congress LC-DIG-ppmsca-72119)

Colonel Frederick G. D'Utassy stands at the centre of his staff with hat in hand; Lieutenant Colonel Alexander Repetti is to his left. The two enlisted men posted either end of the officers also wear full dress. The man at right holds one of the guide flags presented to each company of the 39th New York Infantry (Garibaldi Guard) on May 28, 1861. (US Army Heritage and Education Center. MASS-MOLLUS collection – Vol. 73, p. 3638)

This unidentified musician of the 68th New York Infantry wears the white-trimmed chasseur-pattern uniform authorized by New York in 1863. His cap has a non-regulation plain white pompon attached. (Library of Congress LC-DIG-ppmsca-80357)

shoes" (*NYH*, July 21, 1860: 5.2). By May 1861, six companies of this regiment had received kilts as well as plaid pants, although the former were not generally worn in the field.

Prior to First Bull Run, the personnel of the 79th New York State Militia relegated their kilts to garrison duty or dress occasions, and wore plaid or sky-blue trousers. Nevertheless, other veterans recalled fighting in kilts at Fredericksburg, Vicksburg, and Petersburg (*TEW*, May 12, 1911: 15.1 & 3).

In 1863, New York undertook to uniform at its own expense those militia units that elected to accept a state uniform. As a result, an optional single state militia uniform was prescribed for all infantry regiments via General Orders of May 16 of that year, which consisted of two semi-dress patterns, one of chasseur style with short skirts and the other having a short polka-pattern jacket. Both jackets were single-breasted, of dark-blue cloth piped with white, with pointed cuffs, medium-height collar, and nine buttons. Pants worn with either jacket were light blue: with the chasseur-style jacket these were very full and pleated and trimmed around the pockets; with the polka-pattern jacket they were narrower. The cap worn with both uniforms was semirigid, of dark-blue indigo cloth, and piped with white. It carried the small state military seal at the front, and was surmounted by a red, white, and blue pompon.

Although not implemented until 1864, about 5,000 suits were issued in addition to those for regiments whose uniforms had worn out during Federal service. This marked the first time that a state undertook to supply uniforms at its own expense for regiments not assigned to active service, and broke from the old volunteer militia system that required each enlisted man to buy his own clothing.

New York cavalry and light artillery continued to wear the US mounted service jacket, with either the dress cap or black felt hat. The fatigue suits authorized in 1858 continued in use, as did the Pattern 1854 uniform coat.

PENNSYLVANIA

The Commonwealth of Pennsylvania enlisted 227 regiments and 62 companies of infantry, as well as dozens of emergency militia regiments raised to repel threatened Confederate invasions in 1862 and 1863. A total of 23 regiments and 28 companies of cavalry were also mustered, plus four regiments and 24 batteries and companies of artillery (Phisterer 1883: 14–15). Altogether, 315,017 Pennsylvanians served in the Union Army during the Civil War, of whom 33,183 died in action, or from wounds or disease (Eicher & Eicher 2001: 62).

On April 21, 1858, Pennsylvania passed a militia law establishing that the US Army uniform should be provided for all branches of service, although organizations in existence were permitted to retain their prewar dress. Although this development encouraged the adoption of US Army clothing among newly formed units, there was not enough time before April 1861 for the militia law to have any significant impact on the uniforms worn by volunteer units during the war.

On April 12, 1861, the State Military Establishment of Pennsylvania was re-organized and militia officer Reuben C. Hale was appointed Quartermaster General with the rank of lieutenant colonel (*PI*, April 20, 1861: 4.4). As the state was required to clothe its troops, Governor Andrew G. Curtin sent agent Robert L. Martin to Philadelphia to provide uniforms for 10,000 Pennsylvania troops. By April 23, Martin had established a "uniform manufactory" at the Girard House, a recently vacated hotel in the city. From this establishment, each volunteer was to receive "One cap, one overcoat, one pair shoes, one blue army blouse, one pair pants, two merino shirts, two pair canton flannel drawers, two pair woolen stockings" (*PI*, May 8, 1861: 2.6). Within four days about 23,000 garments had been produced by 30 cutters and 525 female workers employed sewing at the Girard House factory, with the help of several thousand outworkers. On May 10, the *Philadelphia Inquirer* reported that 10,000 suits of clothes had been completed and supplied (*PI*, May 10, 1861: 2.6).

Regarding the provision of uniforms for the remaining 15,000 Pennsylvania volunteers gathering at other military encampments throughout the state, the Quartermaster General's office at Harrisburg next adopted the contract system and advertised on May 1, 1861, for "15,000 Great Coats. 15,000 Army Blouses, Indigo Blue or Cadet Grey, 15,000 Pairs Trousers, 15,000 Undress Caps. 30,000 Flannel or Knit Woolen Shirts. ... [&] 15,000 Pairs Bootees," all of which had to be "army pattern, and conform strictly to the regulation of the United States army, in quality of material and finish" (*PDT*, May 2, 1861: 2.6). By May 21, 1861, contracts had been issued for "Overcoats, Blouses and Pantaloons" to clothiers and hatters in Philadelphia. Two days later, further contracts were advertised for "12,000 Pairs brown linen trousers, undress," plus the same numbers of Army blankets, metallic letters and numbers, and 500 sergeant's sashes (*PDT*, May 24, 1861: 2.5).

Much of the clothing issued during April–May 1861 was of poor quality, but it was not until toward the end of May that this came to the attention of Governor Curtin, who immediately dispatched Special Commissioners Benjamin Haywood and Jacob Fry, Jr., to Washington, DC, to investigate the condition of the Pennsylvania regiments there. During their investigations, Haywood and Fry established that a contract

Louis E, Fagan was a 20-year-old clerk from Philadelphia when he enrolled in the Anderson Troop, originally established as a headquarters guard for Brigadier General Robert Anderson, hero of the defense of Fort Sumter, South Carolina, in April 1861. Fagan wears a Pascal-pattern "Havelock" hat embellished with a small circular patch within which are the letters "RA" (Anderson's initials), a large die-struck brass "crossed sabers" insignia, a black ostrich feather plume, and worsted hat cord that was probably red or orange to match the unusual trim on his mounted service jacket. His mounted service trousers have a reinforced seat and inner leg. (Author's collection)

Enlisting as a private in Co. C, 149th Pennsylvania Volunteer Infantry, Franklin W. Lehlman was wounded at Gettysburg on July 1, 1863. He was transferred to the 18th Regiment, Veteran Reserve Corps, and honorably discharged on June 29, 1865. (Library of Congress LC-DIG-ppmsca-52227)

RIGHT
Cut in the style of the Pattern 1854 mounted service jacket but with non-regulation faded red or orange trim, jackets of this type were worn by the Anderson Troop and 15th Pennsylvania Cavalry. The 1st and 2d Maine Cavalry wore similar jackets, but with yellow trim. (Military & Historical Image Bank CWu6ds)

FAR RIGHT
The jacket worn by the 23d Pennsylvania Volunteer Infantry (Birney's Zouaves) was minus the *tombeaux*, but incorporated triple loops at the lower edge and single loops on the cuffs. (Smithsonian NMAH AF.24942.01)

had been issued by Charles M. "Bucky" Neal, a Philadelphia lawyer and Special Agent of Governor Curtin, to a Pittsburgh business concern called Frowenfeld & Morganstern for $22,385 worth of uniforms (*PDG*, June 15, 1861: 3.1). As a result, Frowenfeld & Morganstern, and Neal, were indicted on June 16, 1861, for fraud in furnishing inferior clothing (*PDG*, June 17, 1861: 3.1).

Meanwhile, President Lincoln issued his first call for three-year volunteers on May 3, 1861, and required 42,034 men amounting to 40 regiments. Although the allotted share for Pennsylvania was ten regiments, the state had already exceeded this and the general government was reluctant to accept any more. Nevertheless, four additional Pennsylvania regiments, the 26th–29th, were accepted during this period.

Determined to utilize its remaining undesignated volunteers, Pennsylvania raised a new state force called the "Reserve Volunteer Corps of the Commonwealth" or, more commonly, the "Pennsylvania Reserve Corps." Constituted on May 15, 1861, this consisted of 13 regiments of infantry, one of cavalry, and one of artillery, with an aggregate strength of 15,856 officers and men. The law creating the Pennsylvania Reserve Corps stipulated that it would be subject at all times to a call by the general government, and this came during the alarm following the Union disaster at First Bull Run. All 15 regiments were mustered-in for three years and passed out of state control, being given a state, as well as reserve, designation. Hence, the 1st–13th Reserves became the 30th–42d Pennsylvania Volunteer Infantry.

Regiments of the Pennsylvania Reserve Corps were in receipt of their uniforms by July 1861, which consisted of "two suits, one – full dress – of light blue army cloth and trousers," and the other of dark-blue four-button sack coats and "brown duck trowsers" (*TCS*, July 13, 1861: 2.5 & 6). Because they wore a bucktail on their caps as a trophy of their marksmanship, the 42d Pennsylvania Volunteer Infantry, also known as the 1st Pennsylvania Rifles, became known as the Bucktails. Adopting the same addition to their headgear, the 149th Pennsylvania Volunteer Infantry was dubbed the Second Bucktails.

"Havelock" hats patented by master hatter Charles L. Pascal and produced by Sullender & Pascal, of Philadelphia, were popular among

Pennsylvania troops, and were worn by the 2d, 6th (Rush's Lancers), and 15th Pennsylvania Cavalry, plus the Anderson Troop. Shaped like a fatigue cap, the "Havelock" hat had a visor, plus a strap and buckle in front. Flaps attached around its sides and back could be folded down to protect the neck, with a brass catch that locked the flaps in either position.

A steady demand for more troops for three years' service followed the mustering-in of the Pennsylvania Reserve Corps, and by the end of 1861 the total number of infantry regiments raised in Pennsylvania amounted to 108, while 13 cavalry regiments and two artillery regiments had been formed, plus various reserve and home-defense regiments. At least eight of these units, or parts of them, and those that followed during the next two years, wore Zouave, or semi-Zouave, uniforms at various times.

The 72d Pennsylvania Volunteer Infantry, or Philadelphia Fire Zouaves, was formed during July–August 1861 from returning three-month volunteers plus recruits from the fire companies of Philadelphia. Acquired from clothiers Rockhill & Wilson of Philadelphia, their clothing consisted of a dark-blue chasseur-pattern cap trimmed with red cord; dark-blue Zouave jacket embellished with brass ball buttons; light-blue pullover shirt with placket front fastened by eight mother-of-pearl buttons, either side of which ran looped red trim; sky-blue trousers with narrow red seam stripes; and white canvas gaiters.

The 76th Pennsylvania Volunteer Infantry, or Keystone Zouaves, was composed of previously independent companies such as the Lawrence Zouaves, Sharon Zouaves, and Curtin Zouaves. When organized during September 1861, this regiment wore a uniform of "handsome army cloth" consisting of a "dark blue cap and jacket, light blue pantaloons, and leather leggings, all in the Zouave style" (*PI*, September 4, 1861: 1.6). Based on photographic evidence, this uniform included a plain blue Zouave jacket with broad, light-colored facings around the edges and cuffs, underneath which was worn a plain pullover shirt with placket front fastened by three or four small buttons. Sky-blue pants varied in style and cut. Headgear was a mixture of forage caps and tasseled fezzes. By the beginning of February 1862, this regiment wore the chasseur uniforms acquired from France.

Upon departure from Philadelphia for the front on October 12, 1861, the 95th Pennsylvania Volunteer Infantry, or Gosline's Zouaves, commanded by Colonel John M. Gosline, were "clad in neat blue uniforms, trimmed in red" (*PI*, October 14, 1861: 8.3). A member of the regiment described the uniform as being of

the best material, heavy marine cloth. The jacket, which was of the sacque pattern, was open, and rounded at the waist, and trimmed with broad and narrow scarlet braid. Down each side was a row of brass buttons … The pants were of full length, not so wide as the

This unidentified corporal of the 23d Pennsylvania Volunteer Infantry (Birney's Zouaves) wears an example of the "dark blue army cloth" Zouave uniform ordered from clothiers Rockhill & Wilson of Philadelphia by the Schuylkill Arsenal during the fall of 1861. Although influenced by the uniform worn by the Gymnast Zouaves, it was more elaborately trimmed and had triple seam stripes on chasseur-pattern trousers. Headgear consists of a red fez although dark-blue caps were also worn by this unit. This corporal has a Bowie knife with horn grip and Colt Pocket revolver tucked into his waist belt. (Daniel J. Miller collection)

13

On November 28, 1862, the Philadelphia-based hatters Adolph and Keen were contracted by the Schuylkill Arsenal to make 650 red fezzes with yellow tassels at 99 cents each for the 114th Pennsylvania Volunteer Infantry (*Zouaves D'Afrique*). These were worn with white turbans for full dress. (Smithsonian NMAH AF.24951.03)

regular "Zouave Petticoat," but just wide enough to harmonize with the pleated waist, in broad folds. The over shirt was of Navy flannel, with silver-plated buttons, corresponding with those on the jacket, but several sizes smaller. The cap was the McClellan style, braided with narrow scarlet braid. A pair of leather leggings nearly reaching the knees finished the uniform. (Galloway 1884: 8)

The Collis Zouaves, or *Zouaves D'Afrique*, were recruited by Charles H.T. Collis, ex-sergeant major of the 18th Pennsylvania Infantry (three months' regiment), who was requested to form an independent company of infantry to be "drilled as Voltigeurs in the French army," and "uniformed similarly to the Zouaves D'Afrique" (*PI*, July 25, 1861: 4.4). As originally organized, the Collis Zouaves included volunteers who had seen action in "the Crimean, Italian, and other recent campaigns" (*PI*, August 15, 1861: 8.3). Recruitment began on July 25 and this unit was accepted by the War Department on August 15, at which time Quartermaster General Meigs issued orders that it should wear the uniform of the French Zouaves. After serving as a bodyguard for Major General Nathaniel P. Banks in the Shenandoah Valley, Collis' Zouaves were expanded into a Zouave regiment and designated the 114th Pennsylvania Volunteer Infantry, or *Zouaves D'Afrique*, in 1862.

In order to use surplus French chasseur uniforms purchased earlier in the Civil War, the US Quartermaster Department ordered them to be altered and turned into Zouave uniforms for the 155th Pennsylvania Volunteer Infantry. The surviving uniform worn by Sergeant George W. Porter, Co. B, 155th Pennsylvania Volunteer Infantry, consists of the jacket and pantaloons, red fez trimmed with yellow and a dark-blue tassel, and white leggings. Note the red cloth V Corps badge attached to the trefoil on the jacket's left breast. (Military & Historical Image Bank CWu4ds)

In his history of the 114th Pennsylvania Volunteer Infantry, musician Frank Rauscher wrote: "The uniform adopted for the regiment was precisely like that of the original company – red pants, Zouave jacket, white leggings, blue sash around the waist, and white turban" (Rauscher 1892: 12). Based on surviving clothing and photographic evidence, the dark-blue jacket was edged with red and had sky-blue pointed cuffs piped with red trim. Under the jacket was a dark-blue pullover vest with three or four buttons hidden by a flap edged in red. The red fez was piped at the bottom with thin yellow lace and had a yellow tassel. The fez was embellished with a white turban, usually worn on guard duty but probably not during combat. The waist sash was sky blue. Red pantaloons were trimmed with yellow lace and tucked into tan leather *jambières* (gaiters) worn over white canvas leggings.

The 155th Pennsylvania Volunteer Infantry, the third regiment to form the Zouave Brigade of the 5th Division, V Corps, Army of the Potomac, in 1864, wore the surplus chasseur uniforms purchased from France in 1861. Zouave jackets heavily trimmed with yellow cloth were made from the various parts of these garments. A yellow-trimmed red sash and a red fez with yellow trim and a dark-blue tassel completed the uniform.

By the end of 1861, most of the volunteer regiments of Pennsylvania had gone into US service, which left the state with a severely limited home-defense force against possible Confederate incursions or larger-scale invasion. The first real threat came in early September 1862 when General Robert E. Lee crossed the Potomac River to begin the Antietam Campaign. In response Governor Curtin ordered 50,000 volunteers to rendezvous at Harrisburg and the 1st–25th Militia Infantry regiments were formed. Although not uniformed and poorly armed, almost all of these regiments took the field, but none saw action. Enlisting as a private in the Sigel Guards, which joined the 2d Militia Infantry Regiment, Private David M. Stauffer recalled: "I was provided with a knapsack, haversack and blanket by the State, with a Harper's Ferry musket, altered from flintlock to percussion, and 40 rounds of buck and ball ammunition" (Stauffer n.d.: 11). Overcoming the lack of uniform, Stauffer donned the gray jacket his half-brother Alfred had worn during early Civil War service with the 28th Pennsylvania Volunteer Infantry, and replaced the "regimental buttons" with "rebel" buttons acquired from a Confederate prisoner of war. The consequences of wearing such buttons might have proved fatal if he had been apprehended by regular Union Army troops outside the lines of his regiment (Stauffer n.d.: 12). Following Lee's withdrawal from Maryland the entire militia force was disbanded by September 24, 1862.

The next invasion of Pennsylvania occurred with the Gettysburg campaign of June–July 1863. On June 15, President Lincoln called on the state to provide 50,000 militiamen for six months, and once again a hastily assembled emergency militia was the result. Eleven days later this force assembled at Harrisburg with the numbering in continuation of the 1862 emergency series creating the 26th–60th Militia Infantry regiments. Included in these were elements of the Philadelphia Home Guard and Reserve Brigade as the 20th, 32d, and 33d regiments, plus regiments recruited among the city's commerce and industry. Among the latter were the First and Second Coal regiments as the 40th and 51st regiments; the Merchants' Regiment as the 44th; and the Victuallers' Regiment or 60th. All of these units wore elements of regulation US Army uniforms.

During General Robert E. Lee's invasion of Pennsylvania in summer 1863, the miners and shippers of coal met in Philadelphia and agreed to suspend business and recruit a regiment for state defense. As a result the Coal Regiment, or 40th Pennsylvania Militia Infantry, was formed and assigned to the Department of the Susquehanna as part of the 3d Brigade, 2d Division, with Colonel Alfred M. Day in command. Archilles Wilds enlisted as a corporal in Co. I of this regiment on July 2, and was mustered-out with the rest of the militia infantry in August 1863. Well clothed and armed by the Coal Trade of Philadelphia, he wears a Pattern 1858 hat with the company letter "I" within the loop of the infantry horn and the regimental number "40" above, a four-button sack coat, and plain sky-blue trousers, and is armed with a Springfield Model 1842 musket. (Author's collection)

MASSACHUSETTS

Nicknamed the "Bay State," Massachusetts provided a total of 122,781 soldiers for the Union cause during the Civil War. Of these men, 13,942 were killed in action or died of wounds or disease (Eicher & Eicher 2001: 62). The units raised in Massachusetts consisted of 68 regiments and 45 companies of infantry; five regiments and one battalion of cavalry; four regiments and eight companies of heavy artillery; one battalion and 17 batteries of light artillery; and two companies of sharpshooters (Phisterer 1883: 13).

One week after the surrender of Fort Sumter near Charleston, South Carolina, on April 13, 1861, Massachusetts commissioned Lieutenant Colonel John H. Reed as Quartermaster General, and one of his immediate tasks was to provide the state volunteers with uniforms and headgear suitable for war service. As a result, a fatigue uniform of gray flannel was chosen, partially because of its availability and also because gray was considered by many to be the appropriate color for state troops. The jacket chosen was of semi-chasseur pattern with a standing collar and shoulder straps, and was edged with red cord. The trousers were matching with narrow red welts on the outer seams. Most of these uniforms were supplied by clothiers Whitten, Hopkins & Co., of Boston. Headgear consisted of gray forage caps with red tops, and a hat invented by Major General Benjamin F. Edmands, of the Massachusetts Volunteer Militia, which had a wide brim that folded up and was buttoned to its crown on four, and in some cases three, sides with strips of vertical red tape trim sewn around each buttonhole.

Several of the Massachusetts regiments organized for three years' service in response to President Lincoln's call for three-year volunteers on May 3, 1861, wore these semi-chasseur gray uniforms. These regiments included the 7th, 9th, and 11th Massachusetts Infantry, while the 1st Massachusetts Infantry was similarly clothed wearing a mixture of militia and state-issue gray semi-chasseur uniforms. Supplied by Haughton, Sawyer & Co., of Boston, the Edmands hat was worn by the 10th Massachusetts Infantry, or Western Regiment, and the 11th Massachusetts Infantry, or Boston Volunteers. This headgear proved unpopular with the men of either regiment, First Lieutenant Joseph K. Newell commanding Co. I, 10th Massachusetts Infantry, writing in his diary: "hats, 'what hats!' of unmentionable dirty, light drab color, that were discarded as soon as caps could be obtained" (Newell 1875: 28).

The wearing of gray inevitably caused confusion and drew friendly fire on Massachusetts volunteers at First Bull Run. Serving in the 1st Brigade of Brigadier General Samuel P. Heintzelman's 3d Division, Army of Northeastern Virginia, Sergeant Gustavus D. Hutchinson, Co. D, 11th Massachusetts Infantry, recorded in his regimental history: "We were dressed in our new gray uniforms, which had been sent us by the

Private Thomas Green, Co. B, 11th Massachusetts Infantry, wears an example of an Edmands hat and a red-trimmed semi-chasseur-pattern jacket. Green enlisted on June 13, 1861, and was killed in action at Second Bull Run on August 29, 1862. (Library of Congress LC-DIG-ppmsca-33339)

State committee … The delusive color cost us dearly, for … one of our own regiments opened fire upon us, mistaking us for Confederates, and several valuable lives were sacrificed" (Hutchinson 1893: 22).

The 2d and 12th Massachusetts Infantry were outfitted in full US Army dress uniforms in blue. Although efforts were made to have gray uniforms adopted by the former regiment, Colonel George H. Gordon was determined that blue should be worn. As a result, Whiting, Galloupe, Bliss & Co., of Boston, were contracted to produce the "uniform of the regular army, cut to fit the form" for "Gordon's Regulars" (Quint 1867: 23). Headgear consisted of the Pattern 1858 dress hat, made by the Boston-based hatter Samuel O. Aborn, "of favorable hat notoriety," which was described as "black Kossuth, turned up on the left side, with black plumes and blue bands" (*BH*, July 8, 1861: 4.5). When the 12th Massachusetts Infantry, or "Webster Regiment," paraded for a flag presentation on July 18, 1861, they wore "the regulation army uniform, with forage caps" (*BDA*, July 19, 1861: 4.1).

Following McClellan's order during August 1861 that no more gray-clad regiments were wanted, the 13th–31st Massachusetts Infantry were issued Federal-style uniforms that included dark-blue uniform coats and sack coats, and either gray or sky-blue pants. Subsequent units recruited were supplied with uniforms and headgear more closely patterned on US Army dress regulations. Despite this, several Massachusetts volunteer companies entered service in three-year regiments wearing Zouave uniforms purchased by the state from private contractors. Boston clothier R.A. MacKenzie provided 98 "Zouave Suits" and 98 "Zouave Caps and Tassels"; William H. Burbeck & Co. of Boston supplied 101 "Uniform Suits, Zouave"; and G.W. Simmons & Co. of the same city provided 101 pairs of "Zouave Trousers," 98 "Zouave vests," 199 "Leggins," and 98 "Sashes" (Schouler 1861: 5, 7, & pullout Table A).

This unidentified soldier wears the first uniform of the Mounted Rifle Rangers of the Massachusetts volunteers. His light-colored Whipple-pattern "Havelock" hat made by the Seamless Clothing Manufacturing Company, of New York City, has the brass letters "MRR" (Mounted Rifle Rangers) at front. His overcoat with cuff-length cape is of the mounted service pattern. (Author's collection)

Identified as being either Joseph N. or William R. Tibbetts, this Zouave wears the uniform adopted by the Boston Light Infantry, or 2d Battalion Riflemen, Massachusetts Volunteer Militia, in July 1861. His headgear was described as a Turkish turban. His jacket was dark blue faced with elaborate orange trimmings edged with gilt ball buttons, underneath which was a red shirt with smaller ball buttons down its front. Pantaloons were also dark blue trimmed with orange braid, and leggings were white canvas. On August 7, 1862, the 2d Battalion was expanded into the 43d Massachusetts Volunteer Militia and served for nine months. (Library of Congress LC-DIG-ppmsca-71065)

Commanded by Captain Ansel D. Wass, an ex-member of the United States Zouave Cadets recruited in Chicago, Illinois by Elmer E. Ellsworth, the Tiger Fire Zouaves were mainly recruited among the firemen of Boston and joined the 19th Massachusetts Infantry as Co. K on August 9, 1861. This company wore "a complete Zouave uniform," received after their arrival in Washington, DC, which was described as "without a particle of red about it, the jacket being dark and the pants and shirts of light blue" (*BET*, June 3, 1861: 2.3). The jacket was also embellished with small brass ball buttons, possibly after that worn by the United States Zouave Cadets, and edged and trimmed with light blue. Headgear was originally a dark-blue fez, but these were replaced by forage caps. The rest of the uniform included a tight-fitting dark-colored vest, waist sash, and yellow leather leggings (*BET*, June 3, 1861: 2.3). Organized in December 1861, the Boston Fire Zouaves (Co. I), 30th Massachusetts Infantry, also known as the Eastern Bay State Regiment, adopted the same pattern of Zouave-style uniform.

One of the best-drilled militia units in Massachusetts, the New England Guard constituted Co. A, 4th Battalion, Massachusetts Volunteer Militia, in March 1861. A second company was organized at that time. On April 24, the 4th Battalion volunteered to garrison the largely unmanned Fort Independence in Boston Harbor, which it did without pay. During September–December 1861, the battalion was expanded and volunteered for three years' service as the 24th Massachusetts Infantry, or New England Guards Regiment, and in 1862 some of its members served for nine months as the 44th Massachusetts Infantry, or 2d New England Guards. By August 1861, the 4th Battalion adopted a chasseur uniform of probable American manufacture, which consisted of a blue coat with yellow trim, yellow shoulder knots, sky-blue pantaloons with yellow trim, white forage cap with yellow piping, and russet leather gaiters (*BET*, August 20, 1861: 3.4). When organized into the 24th Massachusetts Infantry, members of this unit were issued "a substantial uniform" that included "shoes, coats, pants, hats," all of which were probably of Federal pattern (*BH*, September 23, 1861: 1.7).

"Havelock" hats of the type patented by Jonathan F. Whipple, and produced by his Seamless Clothing Manufacturing Company of New York City, were worn by several Massachusetts units that took part in Major General Benjamin F. Butler's New Orleans expedition, including the 4th Battery, Massachusetts Light Artillery, commanded by Captain Charles H. Manning, and the Mounted Rifle Rangers. Made of a seamless piece of light-blue felt, this headgear had a brim or "cape" running around the back and sides for the protection of the head and neck, while a leather visor covered the front and kept the hat in shape. Recruited by Captain S. Tyler Read, the Mounted Rifle Rangers received their "Havelock" hats with the brass letters "MRR" (Mounted Rifle Rangers) at front, plus overcoats, on November 28, 1861 (*BDA*, November 29, 1861: 1.8). Re-organized as a three-company battalion, the Mounted Rifle Rangers were merged into the 3d Massachusetts Cavalry on January 2, 1862, and served with Butler in Louisiana.

NEW JERSEY

Providing 67,500 volunteers for the Union cause, New Jersey organized 38 regiments and four companies of infantry, three cavalry regiments, and five independent batteries of light artillery (Phisterer 1883: 14). Generally, these men fought in the Eastern Theater of the war, with more than one-quarter serving in the Army of the Potomac. Of these men, 5,754 New Jerseyans died either in battle or of disease (Eicher & Eicher 2001: 54 & 62).

The 1st–3d New Jersey Infantry were outfitted entirely with state clothing supplied by contract and delivered to the State Arsenal at Trenton. Uniforms issued to these regiments included a coat with light-colored trim on the bottom edge only of the collar. The same trim edged the non-regulation shoulder straps and came to less of a point on the cuffs compared to Federal-pattern coats.

The 4th–9th New Jersey Infantry were also clothed by the state, as were the 1st New Jersey Cavalry and artillery organized in 1861. Uniform coats issued to the infantry regiments likely conformed more closely to Federal regulations, with trim around the collar and cuffs. Designated as a rifle regiment, the 9th New Jersey Infantry wore green trim rather than the customary infantry sky blue, and was eventually armed with Springfield Model 1861 rifled muskets. Coats supplied to the 1st New Jersey Cavalry also had trimmed shoulder straps and skirts that were shorter than regulation. The 10th New Jersey Infantry was entirely outfitted by the Federal government, but thereafter the state assumed responsibility for clothing all regiments prior to their muster into Federal service, plus all later replacements filling their ranks. Replacement of worn-out uniforms after that was the responsibility of the central government.

In 1861, Quartermaster General Lewis Perrine established a clothing department in the State Arsenal, which produced sack coats and shirts, while large stocks of uniforms were procured both by contract from clothiers Halsey, Hunter & Co., and N. Perry & Co., of Newark, and from the Federal Quartermaster Department. By December 1, 1863, the Clothing Department held among other items:

> 5,045 army hats, felt, trimmed; 4,438 forage caps … 4,146 great coats, infantry light blue; 317 great coats, cavalry; 12,004 uniform coats, infantry, dark blue; 51 uniform coats, musician, dark blue; 75 uniform jackets, cavalry … 801 blue flannel sack coats, lined; 2,348 blue flannel sack coats, not lined; 2,927 pairs trowers, light blue infantry; 1,750 pairs trowers, dark blue infantry; 490 pairs trowers, light blue reinforced … 5,436 pairs bootees. (Perrine 1864: 25)

Issued to both three-year and nine-month volunteers, much of this clothing was patterned after Federal regulations, and presumably the dark-blue "trowers" were left over after the issuance of General Orders No. 108 of December 16, 1861, authorizing their replacement with light blue.

Clothing supplied to three late-war New Jersey regiments varied from the regulation uniform. Seeking to stimulate recruitment, in 1863 Perrine

This unidentified New Jersey volunteer wears a state-pattern uniform coat of the type issued to at least the 1st New Jersey Infantry. (Author's collection)

This unidentified private of the 35th New Jersey Infantry, or Cladek Zouaves, wears the Hawkins' Zouave uniform supplied by the US Clothing Department in New York City. (Library of Congress LC-DIG-ppmsca-70280)

Worn by the 3d New Jersey Cavalry, or 1st Regiment US Hussars, this hussar-style jacket with yellow cord embellishment earned the unit the nickname "Butterflies." (Smithsonian NMAH ZZ.RSN81816W05)

procured through the US Clothing Department in New York City what was known as the "Hawkins' Zouave uniform" for the 33d and 35th New Jersey Infantry, both of which were being recruited as Veteran Volunteers (Perrine 1864: 4). Based on a uniform worn by the 9th New York Infantry, this consisted of a dark-blue jacket, vest, and full-cut trousers trimmed with maroon. Jackets worn by the 33d New Jersey Infantry had small lace trefoils extending from the top corners near the neck and bottom-front corners at the waist. The pleated trousers had a trefoil pattern of lace extending to about midway between the waist and the knee; the vest had a strip of small ball buttons attached to its front; the waist sash was deep red; and the gaiters were black leather. The chasseur cap was piped and quartered with maroon trim.

The Zouave uniform worn by the 35th New Jersey Infantry, or the Cladek Zouaves after its commander Colonel John J. Cladek, incorporated slight differences including maroon lace either side of the jacket forming a loop leading into a trefoil, known as a *tombeau*. The trousers were dark blue with straight legs. These uniforms were withdrawn from service with the 33d and 35th New Jersey Infantry following a General Order dated September 14, 1864.

A third New Jersey regiment distinctively uniformed was the 3d New Jersey Cavalry, also designated the 1st Regiment US Hussars, the only full-strength hussar regiment in the Union Army to experience extensive Civil War service. Recruited during the first quarter of 1864 in response to President Lincoln's call for 300,000 new volunteers, its personnel wore a uniform designed by its commander, Colonel Andrew J. Morrison, who claimed service with Italian nationalist leader Giuseppe Garibaldi.

Assigned to Major General Ambrose E. Burnside's IX Corps, the showy uniforms worn by the 3d New Jersey Cavalry attracted generals who detached elements of the regiment for orderly, courier, and escort duty. Other soldiers in the IX Corps ridiculed their hussar jackets, which were overloaded with yellow braid. Private John McElroy, an enlisted man in the 16th Illinois Cavalry, recalled that the hussars were derided as "daffodil cavaliers" (McElroy 1870: 434).

Corporal John Reiss, Co. K, and Private Godfrey Lutz, Co. G, 3d New Jersey Cavalry, wear the elaborately trimmed hussar-style jackets of their regiment, although their headgear is of differing types. That at left is of "pillbox" pattern with the addition of a visor and metal wreath insignia with the regimental number "3" at center, while the other is a Pattern 1861 forage cap with "crossed sabers" insignia on top. (Library of Congress LC-DIG-ppmsca-52201)

NEW HAMPSHIRE

Known as the "Granite State," New Hampshire provided 17 regiments and four companies of infantry, two cavalry regiments, one heavy-artillery regiment, and one light-artillery battery for service with the Union Army in the Civil War (Phisterer 1883: 12). Of the 32,930 New Hampshirites who contributed to the war effort, 4,882 were killed in action or died of wounds or disease (Eicher & Eicher 2001: 62).

The 2d New Hampshire Infantry was the first regiment from this state to volunteer for the Civil War, being clothed in the same gray uniform as that worn by the 1st New Hampshire Infantry. This included a gray cap with red band, and red cord around the base of the collar of their tailcoat, as supplied by Boston clothiers Whiting, Galloupe, Bliss & Co., and Whitten, Hopkins & Co. This regiment wore dark-blue four-button sack coats during their action at First Bull Run.

Also originally uniformed in gray, the 3d New Hampshire Infantry wore frock coats and trousers of doeskin cloth supplied by clothiers Lincoln & Shaw, of Concord. Blue flannel fatigue blouses for this regiment were procured from Samuel A. & Benjamin F. Haley's Tailoring Establishment of Newmarket. For headgear they initially wore "Havelock" caps designed by Charles F. Brooks, a member of the State Military Committee of the Governor's Council. Made by hatters Purinton & Ham, of Dover, this was described as "a soft-crowned hat of dark brown mixed stuff, with a stiff visor and cape" which protected the back and sides of the neck (*FC*, September 13, 1861: 2.3).

Organized at Manchester during August–September 1861, the 4th New Hampshire Infantry was the first regiment from the state to receive a blue uniform, which consisted of "one pair of pants, one dress coat, one blouse, one light gray overcoat, one woolen and one rubber blanket, together with caps, shoes, stockings, woollen shirts and drawers" (*NHP*, October 2, 1861: 2.1). The dark-blue dress coat and sky-blue pants were also produced by Lincoln & Shaw. Although based on the Pattern 1854, these coats were poorly made with plain collar and cuffs, but with sky-blue trim around non-regulation shoulder straps. The regiment's four-button sack coats were made by Haley's Tailoring Establishment. This regiment also wore "Havelock" hats produced by Purinton & Ham. Overcoats were made by Adams B. Cook, of Weare; gray flannel shirts by Joseph W. Thorpe, of Hillsborough; poncho blankets by Warde, Humphrey & Co., of Concord; and shoes by the workshop in the State Prison (*NHS*, September 7, 1861: 2.5).

Although the 5th New Hampshire Infantry was to be "a Light Infantry Regiment, armed, uniformed and equipped precisely like the Regular Army" (*NHS*, August 31, 1861: 3.1), it also received inferior-quality Lincoln & Shaw uniform coats and "Havelock" caps by Purinton & Ham. Enlisting as a first sergeant in Co. K of this regiment on October 12, 1861, Thomas L. Livermore recalled that the headgear "would do in a row to keep blows from the head and was good to protect the neck from rain, yet in summer it was a sweltering concern" (Livermore: 1920: 27).

This unidentified New Hampshire volunteer wears the gray uniform and cap issued to the 2d New Hampshire Infantry at the beginning of the Civil War. The photographer has correctly applied red paint to the band of the cap, but omitted to add this to the narrow trim at the bottom of the collar of the volunteer's tailcoat. He holds an Allen & Wheelock revolver and is armed with a Springfield Model 1842 musket with socket bayonet. (Daniel J. Binder collection)

The 6th New Hampshire Infantry was mustered-in on November 27, 1861, and received the same pattern of uniform as the 5th New Hampshire Infantry. Havelock-style headgear supplied for the 6th New Hampshire Infantry by Purinton & Ham was likely in response to complaints about the first version, and consisted of an orthodox forage cap but with a stiffened leather visor curved around the rear and sides. A newspaper report stated: "the Government has properly decided to do away with that abomination – the wide awake hat with tucked up brim – and to substitute it with a neat cap with extended horizontal visor" (*DM*, February 21, 1862: 2.4).

Although raised within New Hampshire and credited to that state, the 7th New Hampshire Infantry was organized upon the request of Adjutant General Joseph C. Abbott by direction of the War Department in Washington, DC, under the date of September 2, 1861. Organized at Manchester and mustered-in on December 13, 1861, this regiment received its clothing, arms, and equipment from the central government. Precisely like that of the regular Army, this was sent direct from Washington, DC. The regimental historian Henry F.W. Little described the headgear and clothing as consisting of "'keg hats' of black felt, trimmed with feathers and brasses, dark blue dress coats, dark blue trousers, light blue overcoats, dark blue blouses, and dark blue fatigue caps, the trimmings and chevrons of light blue, except the dark blue on the overcoats" (Little 1896: 14–15). The 8th New Hampshire Infantry received the same pattern of uniform coat as the 4th–6th New Hampshire Infantry, plus second-pattern Purinton & Ham hats.

As the Civil War progressed, the New Hampshire volunteers of 1861 were re-clothed with uniforms more closely based on regulation Union Army pattern, some of which were provided by New York and Philadelphia suppliers. Writing to his brother on New Year's Day, 1862, a member of Co. B, 2d New Hampshire Infantry stated: "The regiment has just been decked out in the regulation coats which is the first time we have had them. They are dark blue frock coats, and not over and above becoming, yet when the reg't is together with equipments on, they looked very well" (*ID*, January 9, 1862: 2.7).

RIGHT
Corporal Mark Robertson, Co. D, 6th New Hampshire Infantry, wears the second-pattern "Havelock" cap with stiff visor at the back and front made by Purinton & Ham. His non-regulation coat with a plain collar and piped shoulder straps was produced by Lincoln & Shaw. The photographer has attempted to color his rank chevrons light blue. Aged 20, Robertson was killed at Second Bull Run. (Author's collection)

FAR RIGHT
Photographed in 1861, 19-year-old Private Arthur H. Perkins, Co. I, 5th New Hampshire Infantry, wears a coat of "shoddy" flannel supplied to his regiment by merchant tailors Lincoln & Shaw, of Concord. On the table by his side, his "Havelock" cap has pinned at its front a small "looped horn" insignia with the regimental number "5" inset and the company letter "I" above. Perkins was appointed second lieutenant on November 1, 1863, and was honorably discharged on November 6, 1864, returning to his home in Danebury, New Hampshire. (Author's collection)

On January 9, 1862, the 3d New Hampshire Infantry assembled for dress parade in their new blue uniforms. Three days later, a member of Co. B wrote: "Our new coats are of a blue cloth, and of very good quality; the regiment looks one hundred per cent better than what it did before it had them" (*ENRA*, January 27, 1862: 2.4). By mid-February 1862 the inferior-quality coats and pants of the 8th New Hampshire Infantry had been replaced, as on February 12 a soldier known only as "Sam" wrote: "We got all our new clothes and they are as smooth as cat fur" (quoted in Stanyan 1892: 53).

While the 1st–8th New Hampshire Infantry became known as "the old regiments," the state organized nine more infantry regiments during 1862–64. At least five of these may also have been uniformed by the state as, on August 18, 1862, State Adjutant General Anthony Colby advertised for proposals for making "Five Thousand and Fifty Three uniform Coats," and the same number of "pairs of Trowsers" (*ID*, August 21, 1862: 4.8). Within ten days, contracts for about 5,000 uniform coats had been awarded to Benjamin Haley and Abraham Thorpe, while the same quantity of trousers was to be produced by Lincoln & Shaw. According to photographic evidence these regiments received regulation-pattern uniforms, although some uniform coats were supplied without infantry trim.

During February 1862, commercial-grade forage caps began to be issued with these uniforms. On February 11, a letter from an enlisted man of the 5th New Hampshire Infantry stated: "We have just received some new fatigue caps, and some scales for the shoulder. They are made of brass and made to look dressy, which indeed they do. The caps are of rather better quality than regiments in general get" (*MDM*, February 11, 1862: 2.4). Later in 1862, a soldier in the same regiment recalled that a Confederate prisoner had asked if the "fellows with a '5' on their caps" (*DWM*, June 14, 1862: 1.6) were sharpshooters.

Beginning with the 9th New Hampshire Infantry, the state-issue caps were adorned with a specially produced set of silver-plated brasses attached to the tops, which were presumably issued upon enlistment of the 9th–15th New Hampshire Infantry during the summer and fall of 1862. The caps displayed a combination of company letter, militia-pattern infantry horn with "simulated embroidery" including cord and tassel, plus the regimental number set inside the loop, and the letters "NHV" (New Hampshire Volunteers). In most cases, all letters were ⅝in. high and numerals were slightly less than ½in. in height, as opposed to US regulations, which specified 1in. letters and ¾in. numerals in brass.

All New Hampshire artillery units wore regulation heavy- or light-artillery uniforms, while New Hampshire cavalry, including the battalion attached to the "First New England Regiment of Cavalry," wore regulation mounted service jackets.

Distinctive silver-plated cap brasses attached to state-issue commercial-grade forage caps are depicted in images of enlisted men of the 9th–15th New Hampshire Infantry. Issued on enlistment during the summer and fall of 1862, the caps usually displayed the company letter above and "NHV" (New Hampshire Volunteers) below, and a Pattern 1858 infantry "looped horn" insignia with numeral(s) representing the regimental number set inside the loop. This unidentified fifer belonged to Co. I, 11th New Hampshire Infantry. (Library of Congress LC-DIG-ppmsca-74716)

RHODE ISLAND

This youthful unidentified volunteer of the 2d Rhode Island Infantry wears the plain enlisted man's pullover blouse designed by Colonel (later Major General) Ambrose E. Burnside and fastened with three small brass buttons on its placket front. The volunteer's plain blue forage cap rests on the table by his side, and a Pattern 1839 oval "US" plate fastens his belt. (Author's collection)

The smallest state in the Union, Rhode Island furnished eight infantry regiments, plus two companies of unassigned infantry; three regiments and one squadron of cavalry; two regiments of heavy artillery; and one regiment and one battery of light artillery to the Union cause (Phisterer 1883: 15). Of the 19,521 Rhode Islanders who served in the Union Army, 621 died in combat, while 1,487 died of other causes such as disease, accidents, and drowning (Grandchamp 2019: 205).

The 2d Rhode Island Infantry was the first regiment from this state organized in response to President Lincoln's call for three-year volunteers issued on May 3, 1861. Based on that supplied to the 1st Rhode Island Detached Militia, the uniform included a dark-blue pullover blouse designed by Colonel (later Major General) Ambrose E. Burnside, gray trousers, and headgear resembling the Pattern 1858 hat but with a taller crown and curled brim. The blouse had a falling collar and placket front opening, and was double-breasted for field and staff officers and single-breasted for line officers and enlisted men. For the latter the blouse was closed by three small brass state buttons, and also had a breast pocket closed by a single button of the same type. Cut full and gathered at the cuff, the sleeves were also fastened by a single small state button. Dark-blue chasseur-pattern forage caps were worn for fatigue purposes. Red poncho-style blankets were worn over the shoulder as a blanket roll.

Following action at First Bull Run, in which the 2d Rhode Island Infantry sustained 98 killed, wounded, and missing, including Colonel John S. Slocum among the fatalities, the regiment was issued "new pants, and those who needed supplied with new blouses" on August 28, 1861 (*PDJ*, September 2, 1861: 2.3). During the fall of 1861, the regiment received new uniforms patterned on US Army regulations. Although of regulation pattern, the frock coats received lacked piping on the collar and cuffs.

Upon organization at Camp Ames during August 12–16, 1861, the 3d Rhode Island Infantry, which contained several Irish companies including the Jackson Guards, Emmett Guards, and Montgomery Guards, was also issued with Burnside-pattern blouses, gray pants, and blue caps. Following its departure from Providence for the front on September 7, 1861, this regiment was ordered via New York City to Fortress Monroe, Virginia, where, during October, it laid aside its state clothing, except for fatigue duty, and "drew blue pants and coats, and donned the genuine regulation fatigue caps common to most of the troops" (Denison 1879: 38–39). This regiment was re-organized as the 3d Rhode Island Heavy Artillery at Hilton Head, South Carolina, on December 19, 1861.

Organized at Camp Greene, on the Pawtuxet River, during September 1861, the 4th Rhode Island Infantry was reported on September 14, 1861, to be wearing "the blue tunic [or Burnside blouse] at present, as a fatigue dress, and blue pants," although it was to be "fully uniformed in accordance with U.S. Army Regulations" (*PDP*, September 14, 1861: 2.6). On October 16, 1861, 1,000 overcoats for this regiment were forwarded from Providence to Washington, DC (*NM*, October 19, 1861: 2.1). This was the only Rhode Island regiment required to pay for its state-issue uniforms, the money being drawn from its wages and clothing allowance despite a near-revolt in its ranks.

First Sergeant William R. Burgess wears the uniform issued to the 7th Rhode Island Infantry in 1863, which included a plain dark-blue jacket with nine-button front. (Robert Grandchamp collection)

(continued on page 33)

NEW YORK

1: Sergeant, 13th New York Infantry, 1861
1a: New York button
2: Private, 7th New York Cavalry, 1863
3: Private, 140th New York Infantry, 1864
3a: V Corps badge

A

PENNSYLVANIA

1: Private, 5th Regiment, Pennsylvania Reserve Corps, 1861
2: Private, Anderson Body Guard, or Anderson Troop, 1862
2a: Anderson Body Guard hat insignia
3: Private, Co. A, 76th Pennsylvania Volunteer Infantry, 1861

MASSACHUSETTS

1: First Sergeant, 1st Massachusetts
Infantry, 1861
1a: Union cockade
2: Private, Co. K, 19th Massachusetts
Infantry, 1863
3: Private, 1st Company, Mounted Rifle
Rangers, Massachusetts Volunteers, 1862

C

3a

3

2

1

D

NEW HAMPSHIRE
1: Corporal, Co. F, 3d New Hampshire Infantry, 1861
2: Private, Co. G, 6th New Hampshire Infantry, 1862
2a: 6th New Hampshire Infantry canteen
3: Musician, Co. A, 15th New Hampshire Infantry, 1863
3a: 15th New Hampshire Infantry cap badge

E

RHODE ISLAND
1: Musician, 2d Rhode Island Infantry, 1861
2: Private, 1st Rhode Island Light Artillery, 1862
2a: Rhode Island state button
3: Private, Co. H, 10th Rhode Island Infantry, 1861

CONNECTICUT, VERMONT, AND MAINE
1: Corporal, 1st Connecticut Heavy Artillery, 1862
1a: Connecticut state button
2: Private, Co. H, 2d Vermont Infantry, 1861
2a: Vermont state button
3: Farrier, 1st Maine Cavalry, 1864

DELAWARE, MARYLAND, AND DISTRICT OF COLUMBIA
1: First Sergeant, 1st Battalion Delaware Cavalry, 1863
2: Private, Co. C, 1st Regiment Potomac Home Brigade, Maryland Cavalry, 1861
3: Corporal, 1st Regiment, District of Columbia Cavalry, 1864
3a: Shield on saddle pommel

Recruitment for the five-company "Burnside Rifle Battalion," which expanded into the 5th Rhode Island Infantry and mustered-in on December 27, 1862, began in Providence during November 1861 (*NM*, November 23, 1861: 3.3). This unit was issued with blue Burnside-pattern blouses and blue caps, but wore "the regulation uniform" when it left for the front on January 4, 1862 (*NM*, January 4, 1862: 3.2). It was re-organized into the 5th Rhode Island Heavy Artillery Regiment in July 1863 (*PEP*, December 27, 1861: 3.7). Subsequent Rhode Island infantry regiments were mainly clothed by the US Quartermaster Department in regulation uniforms. Two exceptions were the 7th Rhode Island Infantry, which received dark-blue, nine-button jackets in 1863, and the Burnside Zouaves.

This unidentified Rhode Island volunteer wears the uniform issued by the state to the 1st Regiment Rhode Island Light Artillery in 1861. This included a dark-blue, nine-button mounted service jacket, and forage cap, trimmed with scarlet. He has a two-piece Pattern 1839 "US" plate on a brown buff leather belt and holds a Model 1840 enlisted artillery saber. His buttons appear to be of the pattern worn by the Providence Marine Corps of Artillery. (Daniel J. Binder collection)

Following the suggestion that "a corps of Zouaves" be formed in Providence on April 22, 1861, the Burnside Zouaves were organized in June of that year (*PDJ*, April 22, 1861: 2.2). Parading when the 1st Rhode Island Infantry returned to Providence on July 28, 1861, the Burnside Zouaves wore "loose flowing scarlet trousers, yellow [*sic*] stripes down the side," with jackets "of blue with yellow [*sic*] trimming," and a red fez with a blue tassel (*PDP*, July 29, 1861: 2.2). This uniform was further described in a later regimental history as "a blue jacket, trimmed with orange, full red pants, gathered at the ankle, with a drab gaiter, a blue mixed undershirt, faced with red, and a white foraging cap, trimmed with red" (Spicer 1892: 40). The Burnside Zouaves served for three months in 1862 as one of the newly formed "National Guard" units making up the 10th Rhode Island Infantry, and performed garrison duty at Washington, DC, receiving instruction in heavy-artillery drill until mustered-out on August 25, 1862.

Regarding Rhode Island artillery, the Providence Marine Corps of Artillery, which subsequently helped recruit and staff nine other light-artillery companies, also initially received the state's Burnside over-shirt, black felt hat, and red poncho-style blankets in 1861. When serving as the 10th Rhode Island Light Artillery Battery in 1862 they wore dark-blue, nine-button mounted service jackets, and forage caps, with scarlet trim. Between August 1861 and January 1862 seven more light-artillery batteries were organized to form the 1st Regiment Rhode Island Light Artillery, all of which are believed to have received state clothing. When Battery B was mustered-in on August 13, 1861, the men were issued Rhode Island uniforms described by Sergeant John H. Rhodes as consisting of "reinforced pants. An outside shirt or tunic, which came down to the knee … A high felt hat with one side turned up, a brass eagle pinned on to hold it, with brass cross cannon in front completed the outfit" (Rhodes 1892: 1–3, 12 & 18). The trousers were originally an almost-black logwood-dyed jean cloth, but their color subsequently faded to a light tan after prolonged exposure to sunlight (Grandchamp 2007: 58).

By November 1861, the whole of the 1st Regiment Rhode Island Light Artillery had received an additional uniform from the state. As worn by the Providence Marine Corps of Artillery, this included the short, nine-button jacket piped in red and partially based on the US Army uniform jacket prescribed for all mounted men since 1854. Also received were sky-blue trousers and dark-blue forage caps. Some men continued to wear their Burnside-pattern shirts until these garments were completely worn out.

Organized at Pawtucket from December 1861 through March 1862, and originally the idea of Governor William Sprague, the "First New England Regiment of Cavalry" contained two battalions of Rhode Islanders and one battalion of New Hampshire troopers, and was issued with "a uniform of the United States regulation pattern" (*FC*, December 26, 1861: 3.6).

CONNECTICUT

A total of 51,937 men from Connecticut served in the Union Army, providing 27 infantry regiments, one cavalry regiment, two regiments of heavy artillery, and three batteries of light artillery (Phisterer 1883: 13). Of these, 5,354 were killed in action or died from wounds or disease (Eicher & Eicher 2001: 62).

A state-pattern uniform was issued to the 4th–13th Connecticut Infantry, and 1st Light Artillery Battery. Based in part on the uniform prescribed for its volunteer militia in 1856, which in turn was based on US Army regulations, it consisted of a dark-blue uniform coat and trousers, plus Pattern 1858 hats and forage caps. Owing to a shortage of dark-blue cloth, personnel of the 4th Connecticut Infantry were supplied gray fatigue jackets, trousers, and caps, but received state blue clothing in October 1861. On arrival in Jersey City, New Jersey, this regiment was described as "thoroughly equipped and uniformed; their dress is that of a National Guard, gray fatigue, with a light gray … cap. The officers are also equipped in the regular army officers' uniform, with the Connecticut State buttons" (*NYH*, June 12, 1861: 8.5).

Branch-of-service trim other than US Army regulation infantry sky blue was worn by several Connecticut units. Green trim was initially applied to the uniforms of flank companies A and B of the 6th Connecticut Infantry, and the whole of the 11th Connecticut Infantry, which was considered a rifle regiment. The latter regiment also initially wore high black leggings.

The 4th Connecticut Infantry was re-designated the 1st Connecticut Heavy Artillery on January 2, 1862, and issued the state-pattern uniform with red branch-of-service trim. Members of the 1st Connecticut Light Artillery wore red trim on their coats and trousers. They were also issued plain dark-blue jackets, and soft drab felt hats.

The 5th Connecticut Infantry left for the front wearing a regimental uniform consisting of light-gray felt hats, "indigo blue coat and pants and army gray overcoats" (*NYH*, July 7, 1861: 8.2). This regiment also appears to have received Federal-style sack coats as, on July 13, it was observed that "blue blouses" were "plenty on the streets" of Hartford when it was granted furlough prior to departure for the war (*CP*, July 13, 1861: 2.7).

Regarding the remaining regiments initially issued state clothing, the 7th Connecticut Infantry left New Haven for Jersey City on September 18, 1861, dressed in "the regular uniform" plus gray overcoats (*NYDT*, September 20, 1861: 8.5). The 8th Connecticut Infantry was initially uniformed in the same fashion minus overcoats, which prompted the comment that a few "wide-awake capes," as worn by paramilitary groups that supported Abraham Lincoln in 1860, might be made available for "the use of the picket guard" (*HDC*, September 24, 1861: 2.4).

Known as the "Irish Regiment" and formed using the Emmett Guard, of New Haven, as its nucleus, the 9th Connecticut Infantry was initially poorly clothed receiving "One suit of blue, of poor material," which constituted "their entire equipment." Stationed for two months at Camp English, in New Haven, their pantaloons began to assume "various degrees of dilapidation" (Croffut 1868: 140). On Thanksgiving Day 1861, this regiment left New Haven for Camp Chase near Lowell, Massachusetts, "numbering about six hundred men, ragged, unarmed, and dispirited" (*HDC*, November 12, 1861: 2.3). The last Connecticut

The frock coat worn by this unidentified Connecticut volunteer has trim around the collar and plain cuffs. His dark-blue trousers possibly indicate that he was photographed before General Orders No. 108, issued on December 16, 1861, required sky-blue trousers to be worn. He holds a plain chasseur-pattern cap. (Author's collection)

infantry regiment to be clothed by the state, the 13th Connecticut Infantry, received dark-blue trousers in place of the regulation sky blue while encamped at New Haven. Originally formed as a single company, the 1st Connecticut Cavalry expanded into a battalion and then a regiment by 1863. Recruits were promised a US Army regulation uniform from the outset.

Until 1864 Connecticut continued to uniform volunteer regiments initially, acting as agent for the Federal government with contracts for "army uniforms" being completed by clothiers such as John H. Cook, of New Haven, and James M. Nelson, of Norwich (*HDC*, January 10, 1862: 2.3). With the exception of state-pattern buttons, after April 1862 the uniforms closely resembled US Army regulations. There were no distinctive uniforms such as Zouave or chasseur volunteers, and Connecticut regiments were noted for the formality of their dress, which included brass shoulder scales and white dress gloves.

VERMONT

Private Lucius Fox, Co. I, 8th Connecticut Infantry, wearing a state-issued untrimmed Pattern 1854 uniform coat with buttons bearing the state coat of arms. He holds a Pattern 1858 dress hat on which he has fixed the hat cord tassels up around the Pattern 1858 infantry "looped horn" insignia at its front. (Daniel J. Binder collection)

A total of 32,549 Vermonters served in the Civil War, with the Green Mountain State fielding 17 infantry regiments, one cavalry regiment, one regiment and one company of heavy artillery, and three light-artillery batteries (Phisterer 1883: 12–13). Vermont suffered a total of 1,832 men killed or mortally wounded in battle, and another 3,405 died of disease, in prison, or from other causes, amounting to a total loss of 5,237. More than 2,200 Vermonters were taken prisoner during the Civil War, and 615 of them died during or as a result of their imprisonment (Peck 1892: vi).

The first two regiments recruited for three years' service from Vermont, the 2d and 3d Vermont Infantry, were clothed in gray uniforms. This included nine-button Federal-pattern frock coats with light-blue trim around the collar, non-regulation gray shoulder straps, and plain gray caps and trousers. On arrival in New York City *en route* for Washington, DC, the 2d Vermont Infantry was reported wearing "a dark gray uniform, substantial and well cut" (*NYH*, June 26, 1861: 4.6). Every man in this regiment wore a sprig of hemlock in his cap in commemoration of the Revolutionary War (1775–83) valor of the original "Green Mountain Boys" (*VP*, June 27, 1861: 2.1). When the 2d Vermont Infantry arrived in New York City, the press reported that their uniforms were of

regulation gray, but there are few of them that fit the men. From the appearance of some of them, which hang sack like over the limbs of the wearer [,] it would seem that the State tailor had thought that the Green Mountain military were veritably Falstaffs in corpulency. The material looks like gray fustian dyed in mud. They were furnished two weeks since, and, such is the counterfeit kersey of which they seem to be made, they are now completely faded and worn-looking. (*VP*, July 4, 1861: 2.7)

Worn into Virginia, the state-issue clothing of the 2d Vermont Infantry caused confusion in the Union Army ranks. An unidentified member of the regiment wrote from near Fairfax Courthouse on July 15, 1861: "Our grey uniform looks similar to the 'Mt. Vernon Guards' [a company of rebels], and the [11th New York] Zouaves came nigh shooting some of us when we first made our appearance; but now they are in our camp and have become so well acquainted with the Vermont Second that they will hereafter know us anywhere" (*WDJ*, July 22, 1861: 2.4).

The 3d Vermont Infantry received their uniforms on July 4, 1861. Once again the state clothing was substandard. A letter from a soldier at Camp Baxter in St. Johnsbury stated: "The uniforms are distributed and are not what the State of Vermont should furnish her soldiers … the cloth does not hold its color, and the light of the sun is fatal to its appearance" (*BFP*, July 12, 1861: 2.3 & 4).

By the beginning of October 1861, both the 2d and 3d Vermont Infantry were "suffering for want of clothing." Writing from Camp Advance near the Chain Bridge, District of Columbia, a member of the recently arrived 4th Vermont Infantry reported: "The 2d do not look so neat and tidy as when in Camp Underwood. Their gray uniforms (which are being replaced by blue) are now dirty and dingy. They look as though they had seen service – and hard service, too" (*BFP*, October 11, 1861: 2.3). Writing from Camp Griffin, Virginia, a man in the 3d Vermont Infantry stated that the uniforms of his regiment were "dirty, rusty, too thin, [and] too shrunk" (*BFP*, November 8, 1861: 2.2).

By October 23, Governor Erastus Fairbanks had received a telegram from Brigadier General William F. Smith, commanding the Vermont Brigade, stating: "They need immediately about 850 blue uniforms, and sixteen hundred pair of pants" (*SADM*, October 23, 1861: 2.1). By November 14, 1861, the 2d and 3d Vermont Infantry had received "new uniforms of army blue," plus blankets and overcoats (Benedict 1886: 137).

The 4th Vermont Infantry was the first regiment to be uniformed in blue from the outset by Vermont. The coats and pants for this regiment, and the 5th Vermont Infantry, were made in Boston, Massachusetts, and overcoats were produced in Rutland, Vermont (*SADM*, October 25, 1861: 2.2). Clothing for the 4th Vermont Infantry was described as "a great improvement over those of the preceding regiments … They are made of all wool cloth of the army blue color; and the hats are of the same style as is now worn in the regular service" (*VP*, September 19, 1861: 2.2). This regiment joined the 2d, 3d, and 5th Vermont Infantry, and later the 6th, forming the Vermont Brigade. Both the 5th and 6th Vermont Infantry also received "blouses and pants, of army blue" supplied by the state (*SADM*, October 14, 1861: 2.3). The 5th Vermont Infantry was hurried off to the front on September 23, 1861, only partly clothed and equipped. According to an account in the Brattleboro press, this regiment did not receive overcoats until mid-October despite the cold and wet weather, and after having been informed that these would be waiting for them on arrival at Washington, DC (*SADM*, October 18, 1861: 2.1).

By the time the 6th Vermont Infantry was organized, the state had learned "a good deal in the business of equipping troops," and from the ampler supplies of Army clothing then available the recruits were uniformed as fast as they arrived (Benedict 1886: 209–10). Mustered into

A resident of Tunbridge, Vermont, 24-year-old Philo Emery enlisted as a private in Co. E, 2d Vermont Infantry, on May 21, 1861. He was wounded in the left knee at the Battle of the Wilderness on May 5, 1864, and died of his wound on June 9, 1864. In this early-war *carte de visite* he wears his first issue uniform, which consists of a plain gray coat with Vermont "state seal" buttons and shoulder straps with smaller buttons of the same pattern. The band on his gray chasseur-pattern cap comes to a peak, which was a distinctive feature of early-war Vermont headgear. (Author's collection)

Federal service at Camp Gregory Smith, Montpelier, on October 15, 1861, the 6th Vermont Infantry left for Washington, DC, four days later, on which occasion it was reported to be "fully uniformed and equipped, and leaves the State better appointed than any Regiment that has preceded it" (*SADM*, October 21, 1861: 2.1).

Recruiting began for the 7th and 8th Vermont Infantry during the winter months of 1861, but these regiments were not fully organized and uniformed by the state in dark-blue frock coats and caps, and sky-blue trousers, until the beginning of 1862. The 9th–17th Vermont Infantry continued to be uniformed at first by the state, following which the US Quartermaster Department looked after their clothing needs. For example, the 9th Vermont Infantry, organized in July 1862, received "the United States regulation uniform, of blue caps, dark-blue jackets [sic] and light-blue trousers" (*BDT*, July 19, 1862: 4.4).

Efforts to raise a regiment of Vermont cavalry began in September 1861 when Lemuel B. Pratt, a wealthy farmer in Colchester, Chittenden County, was issued a commission and instructed to have the unit "ready as soon as possible" (*SADM*, September 12, 1861: 1.5). Reported to "understand horses and men," and knowing "what kind are wanted for both," Pratt soon recruited the ranks to overflowing in all ten companies of what became the first full regiment of cavalry raised in New England. Going into camp at Burlington, the 1st Vermont Cavalry had received

The cut of his uniform and headgear indicates that this unidentified private enlisted in Co. H of either the 2d or 3d Vermont Infantry in 1861. Magnification of the image also reveals that his buttons bear the state seal of Vermont. (Library of Congress LC-DIG-ppmsca-31692)

"stable jackets, haversacks ... and sacks [four-button sack coats]" by October 23, 1861 (*SADM*, October 23, 1861: 3.4).

When provided with the rest of their clothing, about 300 troopers led by Colonel Pratt paraded through the streets of Burlington on November 4, 1861, on which occasion it was reported that they wore "a blue-black regulation hat, and a fatigue cap; jacket of dark blue trimmed with yellow braid and brass buttons, and with brass scales on the shoulder; trousers of light blue; top boots; overcoat of brown cloth, made large and long, with a large cape; stable jacket; canteen; sabre and belt" (*SADM*, November 7, 1861: 2.1 & 4.3).

Promised "the best of Uniforms," the 2d Vermont Battery Light Artillery was issued regulation Federal artillery-pattern clothing and headgear (*BDT*, January 1, 1862: 3.3). Other Vermont artillery units received the same outfit.

MAINE

Furnishing 64,973 men for the Union Army, Maine provided 30 regiments and 16 companies of infantry, two cavalry regiments, one heavy-artillery regiment, one battalion of light artillery, and one sharpshooter battalion (Phisterer 1883: 12). The total number of Mainers killed in action, or who died from wounds or disease, was 9,398 (Eicher & Eicher 2001: 62).

The uniform chosen for the 2d–6th Maine Infantry during the spring of 1861 consisted of a seven-button untrimmed uniform coat, trousers, and forage cap, all of gray cloth. Some of the regiments also wore drab or gray hats. Overcoats were also gray and of US Army regulation pattern. Buttons were generally Maine state pattern and belt plates carried the letters "VMM" (Volunteer Militia of Maine).

The 3d Maine Infantry arrived in Washington, DC, wearing the "army grey uniform throughout," on June 6, 1861 (*LDEJ*, June 12, 1861: 2.3). The 4th Maine Infantry was reported as wearing "substantial grey suits, and equipped with knapsacks" when the regiment passed through Wilmington, Delaware, on June 20, 1861 (*DSJS*, June 21, 1861: 2.6). Three days later, the 5th Maine Infantry received 980 gray "uniform coats" of "Hamilton Doeskin, all wool" plus 930 pairs of pantaloons of "Dexter Doeskin," made at Dexter (*BDWC*, June 18, 1861: 2.4). Headgear for the 5th Maine Infantry consisted of drab hats. When this regiment arrived in Washington, DC, on June 28, 1861, it was described as wearing "light grey pantaloons and coats, and high top, dark grey felt hats, turned up at the sides" (*NR*, June 29, 1861: 3.2).

Prior to departure for the front, the 6th Maine Infantry paraded at Portland on July 4 dressed in "knit frocks, grey pants, and the regulation hat" (*PPH*, July 6, 1861: 2.6). On the regiment's arrival in New York City, each man also had "an extra fatigue uniform, consisting of gray pants and shirt, presented to them by various sewing societies" (*NYH*, July 19, 1861: 8.5). Based on photographic evidence, many members of the 6th Maine Infantry also wore tasseled fezzes.

Maine troops began to be re-clothed in blue during July 1861. According to Corporal Abner R. Small, Co. G, 3d Maine Infantry, on July 3, 1861, his unit received new uniforms consisting of loose blue flannel blouses, looser light-blue pantaloons, and baggy forage caps

Private James B. Holden, Co. H, 1st Vermont Cavalry, wears full dress likely issued to his regiment during November 1861. The "crossed sabers" insignia on the front of his Pattern 1858 hat has his regimental number above and company letter below. His mounted service jacket is trimmed with yellow on the collar and cuffs, and has brass shoulder scales attached. He wears top-boots over his plain sky-blue trousers, and holds a Model 1860 light-cavalry saber. (Library of Congress LC-DIG-ppmsca-74294)

This early-war Maine volunteer wears the state uniform issued to the 1st–6th Maine Infantry during May–July 1861, which consisted of a plain gray coat with a seven-button front, plain gray trousers, and Pattern 1858 forage cap with a wide, light-colored lower band. A gray infantry-pattern overcoat is draped over a small table by his side. He holds at "Order – arms" a Springfield Model 1842 musket with fixed bayonet. He has a small spear-pointed knife with stag-antler handle tucked into his waist belt and a small tin drum canteen on a leather strap over his right shoulder. (Author's collection)

(Small 2000: 8 & 14). Although originally a three-month regiment, the 2d Maine Infantry re-enlisted for two years and received new blue uniforms in early September 1861 while stationed at Fort Corcoran in the defenses of Washington, DC (*BDWC*, September 13, 1861: 2.4). The 5th Maine Infantry received blue uniforms during the same period (*LDEJ*, November 2, 1861: 3.2).

All subsequent infantry regiments enlisted in 1861, consisting of the 7th–15th Maine Infantry, received state-made uniforms of blue cloth. Initially, the 7th Maine Infantry, or Washburn Zouaves, was to "adopt the Zouave dress and drill," but nothing seems to have come of this (*LDEJ*, August 12, 1861: 3.2). When this regiment moved to Baltimore, Maryland, on August 23, 1861, it wore "the blue uniform prescribed by the army regulations" (*OD*, August 30, 1861: 2.5). The 9th Maine Infantry arrived in Boston on September 24 "neatly uniformed in the regular uniform, of dark and light blue, with good, substantial overcoats" (*BDA*, September 25, 1861: 1.8).

Production of clothing for the 7th–9th Maine Infantry had been initiated on July 25, 1861, when Acting Quartermaster General John L. Hodson requested proposals for 1,000–2,000 each of blouses, pairs of trousers, and pairs of brogans, to be delivered in Augusta, Maine, by August 20, 1861. Also required were 2,000–4,000 shirts with "the State furnishing flannel." On the same occasion, the state requested 1,000–2,000 each of knapsacks, haversacks, canteens, "sets Equipments," and "sets Camp Utensils, French Pattern" (*LDEJ*, July 31, 1861: 2.4).

In order to clothe the 10th–15th Maine Infantry, the state requested proposals from contractors for "Coats, Pants, Blouses, Shirts, Drawers, Camp-utensils, Knapsacks, Haversacks, Canteens and Shoes for Infantry Regiments" (*LDEJ*, October 4, 1861: 3.3). Passing through Boston on October 6, 1861, the 10th Maine Infantry, the nucleus of which was composed of former three-month volunteers of the 1st Maine Infantry, wore a "substantial uniform of light blue," indicating that they wore overcoats over their dark-blue coats or blouses (*BH*, October 7, 1861: 2.2).

Organized during 1862–64, the remaining three-year and nine-month regiments, composed of the 16th–32d Maine Infantry, were clothed in regulation uniforms supplied by the US Quartermaster Department. An unidentified member of the nine-month 23d Maine Infantry described the uniform as consisting of a "thick woolen shirt … light blue thick woolen pants, dark blue blouse, stout shoes, and dark blue military cap" (*LDEJ*, November 6, 1862: 2.2).

Eventually holding the unenviable distinction of having the highest battle casualties of any Union Army cavalry regiment in the Civil War, having suffered 174 officers and men killed and wounded, the 1st Maine Cavalry was organized for three years' service at Augusta on October 31, 1861. The day before, it was reported that this regiment would be clothed in regular Army-pattern uniforms with "[dark] blue jacket and pants, trimmed with yellow" (*LDEJ*, October 31, 1861: 3.2). The jacket had unusual narrow yellow trim either side of its 11-button front. The 2d Maine Cavalry wore jackets of the same pattern. Maine artillery units were uniformed in either light or heavy regulation artillery clothing. Formerly the 18th Maine Infantry, the 1st Maine Artillery wore the latter after reorganization in 1863.

DELAWARE

The only slave state not to send units to fight for the Confederacy, Delaware provided nine regiments and four companies of infantry, one regiment and one company of cavalry, two light-artillery batteries, and one heavy-artillery company (Phisterer 1883: 15). A total of 11,236 Delawareans served the Union cause, of whom 882 died either in battle or of disease, while hundreds more returned home wounded or sick. (Eicher & Eicher 2001: 54).

When re-organized for three years' service in September 1861, Cos. A and B of the 1st Delaware Infantry were "costumed *a la* Zouave, blue uniform, red trimmings, fatigue caps and leggings" (*DR*, September 12, 1861: 3.4). The remainder of the regiment received US Army regulation uniforms including frock coat, sack coat, and Pattern 1858 dress hats. Drum-Major Patrick Dooley was outfitted with "the tallest and most gorgeous of shakos, with trimmings to match" (Seville 1884: 30).

During July 1861, the 2d Delaware Infantry received a uniform consisting of an "army blue jacket and dark blue pantaloons" (*DR*, August 1, 1861: 3.4). Formed during the spring of 1862, the 3d Delaware Infantry was issued US Army regulation infantry clothing including forage caps, frock coats, sack coats, greatcoats, and bootees, as were the following six infantry regiments from the state.

Based on Clothing Books of the 1st Battalion Delaware Cavalry, on September 1, 1863, enlisted men were issued with caps, jackets, sack coats, greatcoats, pants, bootees, and shoulder scales. According to photographic evidence, the jackets were 12-button mounted service jackets with the facing color on the collar. They were later replaced by those with more regulation trim, but with only an 11-button front. Organized in 1862 and 1863 respectively, the 1st and 2d Field batteries were amalgamated with the 1st Delaware Cavalry in 1863. In addition to their light-artillery uniforms, recruits for these units received artillery "crossed cannon" insignia for their caps.

John L. Algie enlisted as a private in Co. A, 3d Delaware Infantry, on December 30, 1861. He was transferred to Co. I on May 1, 1862, and re-enlisted as a veteran on March 31, 1864. His regiment was returned to the Army of the Potomac during May 1864 and he was wounded at Hatcher's Run on February 6, 1865. He wears a uniform coat with sky-blue infantry trim, full-dress shoulder scales, and sky-blue trousers. He holds a Springfield Model 1842 musket. (Dr. Michael R. Cunningham collection)

Made by Griswold & Son, of New York City, this late-war forage cap was worn by Private Algie, 3d Delaware Infantry. Attached to its top is a Pattern 1858 horn with the regimental number "3" within the loop, below which is the company letter "I." Above this is a V Corps Maltese cross badge. The 3d Delaware Infantry was attached to the 2d Brigade, 4th Division, V Corps, Army of the Potomac, from May 1864 through June 1865. (Dr. Michael R. Cunningham collection)

Private Jacob E. Myers enlisted for three years in Co. C, 1st Regiment Potomac Home Brigade, Maryland Cavalry, at Gettysburg, Pennsylvania, on August 27, 1861. He wears another example of the non-regulation, eight-button coat with the collar and shoulder straps likely trimmed in yellow, and has a Savage revolver tucked in his belt. (Library of Congress LC-DIG-ppmsca-77729)

MARYLAND

Known as the Old Line State, Maryland formed 20 regiments and one company of infantry, four regiments and four companies of cavalry, and six light-artillery batteries for the Civil War (Phisterer 1883: 15). A total of 33,995 Marylanders served in all branches of the Union Army, of whom 2,982 were killed, or died of wounds or disease (Eicher & Eicher 2001: 62).

Maryland infantry regiments generally received US Army regulation clothing. Recruited on August 30, 1861, the 5th Maryland Infantry received "two suits of uniform, including the regulation hats and caps" by November 18, which indicates that they received dress and fatigue clothing (*BC*, November 20, 1861: 1.7).

The four regiments of the Potomac Home Brigade, and two regiments of the Eastern Shore Home Guard, wore uniforms loosely based on US Army regulations. Regarding the second regiment of the latter organization, the uniforms were reported to be "of army blue cloth, well made, warm, and quite neat in appearance" (*KN*, October 19, 1861: 2.3).

Originally known as the Maryland Border Legion, the Purnell Legion was a mixed command consisting of ten companies of infantry, four companies of cavalry, and two companies of artillery. Recruits were advised that "Clothing, Uniforms, Horses, Arms, Equipments" was to be "on a footing with the Regular Army" (*BC*, September 2, 1861: 2.5; *TCW*, November 7, 1861: 2.1).

DISTRICT OF COLUMBIA

A total of 15,181 men from the District of Columbia served in two regiments and one battalion of infantry, plus one cavalry regiment (Phisterer 1883: 15). Formed in 1863, the cavalry regiment was commanded by Colonel Lafayette C. Baker. Approximately 290 men from the District of Columbia died in battle or as a result of their wounds (Eicher & Eicher 2001: 62). As far as is known, all four of these units wore US Army regulation uniforms.

The 1st District of Columbia Cavalry was formed between June and December 1863 and assigned to special service as scouts in south-eastern Virginia within Brigadier General August V. Kautz's cavalry division of the Army of the James. They wore black slouch hats, dark-blue mounted service jackets with yellow trim, and plain sky-blue trousers. Note the designation "1 DC" in brass numeral and letters on the hat held by the man seated at center right. This illustration was published in *The Photographic History of the Civil War* (Vol. 4, p. 335). (Author's collection)

SELECT BIBLIOGRAPHY

Benedict, George G. (1886). *Vermont in the Civil War*. Vol. 1. Burlington, VT: Free Press Association.

"Communication from the Governor ... April 16, 1861, entitled, 'An Act to Authorise the Embodying and Equipment of a Volunteer Militia and to Provide for the Public Defence,'" State of New York. No. 15. In Assembly, January 9, 1862.

Croffut, W.A. & J.M. Morris (1868). *Military and Civil History of Connecticut during the War of 1861–1865*. New York, NY: L. Bill.

Denison, Frederic (1879). *Shot & Shell: the Third Rhode Island Heavy Artillery Regiment in the War of the Rebellion*. Providence, RI: J.A. Reid.

Eicher, John H. & David J. Eicher (2001). *Civil War High Commands*. Stanford, CA: Stanford University Press.

Galloway, G. Norton (1884). *The Ninety-fifth Pennsylvania Volunteers (Gosline's Pennsylvania Zouaves), in the Sixth Corps*. Philadelphia, PA: no publisher.

Grandchamp, Robert (2007). "'The appearance of a gang of Chinamen:' A Study of the Uniforms Worn by Brown's Battery B, First Rhode Island Light Battery," *Military Collector & Historian* (Spring), Vol. 59, No. 1: 58–61.

Grandchamp, Robert (2019). *Rhode Island's Civil War Dead: A Complete Roster*. Jefferson, NC: McFarland & Co. Inc.

Hutchinson, Gustavus D. (1893). *A Narrative of the Formation and Services of the Eleventh Massachusetts Volunteers*. Boston, MA: Alfred Mudge & Son.

Little, Henry F.W. (1896). *The Seventh Regiment New Hampshire Volunteers in the War of the Rebellion*. Concord, NH: Ira C. Evans, Printer.

Livermore, Thomas L. (1920). *Days and Events, 1860–1866*. Boston, MA: Houghton Mifflin Co.

McElroy, John (1870). *Andersonville: A Story of Rebel Military Prisons*. Toledo, OH: Blade Printing & Paper Co.

Newell, Captain Joseph Keith, ed. (1875). *"Ours." Annals of the 10th Regiment, Massachusetts Volunteers, in the Rebellion*. Springfield, MA: C.A. Nichols & Co.

Peck, Theodore S. (1892). *Revised Roster of Vermont Volunteers*. Montpelier, VT: Watchman Publishing Co.

Perrine, Lewis (1864). *Annual Report of the Quartermaster General of the State of New Jersey for the Year 1863*. Trenton, NJ: Printed at the "True American" Office.

Phisterer, Frederick (1883). *Statistical Record of the Armies of the United States*. New York, NY: Charles Scribner's Sons.

Quint, Alonzo H. (1867). *Record of the Second Massachusetts Infantry, 1861–65*. Boston, MA: James P. Walker.

Rauscher, Frank (1892). *Music on the March, 1862–'65, with the Army of the Potomac, 114th Regt. P.V., Collis' Zouaves*. Philadelphia, PA: Press of Wm. F. Fell.

Schouler, William (1861). *Annual Report of the Adjutant-General, of the Commonwealth of Massachusetts*. Boston, MA: William White, Printer to the State. Containing "Report of the Military Committee of the Council, December 27, 1861."

Seville, William P. (1884). *History of the First Regiment, Delaware Volunteers, from the commencement of the three months service to the final muster-out at the close of the Rebellion*. Wilmington, DE: The Historical Society of Delaware.

Small, Abner Ralph (2000). *The Road to Richmond: The Civil War Letters of Major Abner R. Small of the 16th Maine Volunteers*. New York, NY: Fordham University Press.

Spicer, William Arnold (1892). *History of the 9th & 10th Rhode Island Volunteers, and the 10th Rhode Island Battery, in the Union Army in 1862*. Providence, RI: Snow & Franham.

Stanyan, John M. (1892). *A History of the Eighth Regiment of New Hampshire Volunteers*. Concord, NH: Ira C. Evans, Printer.

Stauffer, David M. (n.d.). "My Life," Box 2, Folder 4, Stauffer Collection, Archives and Special Collections, Martin Library of the Sciences, Franklin & Marshall College, Lancaster, PA.

Todd, Frederick P. (1983). *American Military Equipage 1851–1872*. Vol. 2, "State Forces." New York, NY: Chatham Square Press, Inc.

Todd, William (1886). *The Seventy-Ninth Highlanders, New York Volunteers, in the War of the Rebellion*. New York, NY: Press of Brandow, Barton & Co.

US War Department (1899). *The War of the Rebellion: a Compilation of the Official Records of the Union and Confederate Armies*. Series III, Vol. 1. Washington, DC: Government Printing Office.

Newspapers

Albany Evening Journal, Albany, NY (*AEJ*); *Altoona Tribune*, Altoona, PA (*AT*); *Baltimore Clipper*, Baltimore, MD (*BC*); *Bangor Daily Whig and Courier*, Bangor, ME (*BDWC*); *Boston Daily Advertiser*, Boston, MA (*BDA*); *Boston Evening Transcript*, Boston, MA (*BET*); *Boston Herald*, Boston, MA (*BH*); *Burlington Daily Times*, Burlington, VT (*BDT*); *Burlington Free Press*, Burlington, VT (*BFP*); *Connecticut Press*, Hartford, CT (*CP*); *Daily Evening Traveller*, Boston, MA (*DET*); *Daily Mirror*, Manchester, NH (*DM*); *Daily Union and Advertiser*, Rochester, NY (*DUA*); *Delaware Republican*, Wilmington, DE (*DR*); *Delaware State Journal and Statesman*, Wilmington, DE (*DSJS*); *Daily Union and Advertiser*, Rochester, NY (*DUA*); *Dollar Weekly Mirror*, Manchester, NH (*DWM*); *Evening Star*, Washington, DC (*ES*); *Exeter News-Letter and Rockingham Advertiser*, Exeter, NH (*ENRA*); *Farmer's Cabinet*, Amherst, NH (*FC*); *Hartford Daily Courant*, Hartford, CT (*HDC*); *Independent Democrat*, Concord, NH (*ID*); *Kent News*, Chestertown, MD (*KN*); *Lewiston Daily Evening Journal*, Lewiston, ME (*LDEJ*); *Manchester Daily Mirror*, Manchester, NH (*MDM*); *National Republican*, Washington, DC (*NR*); *New Hampshire Patriot*, Concord, NH (*NHP*); *New Hampshire Statesman*, Concord, NH (*NHS*); *Newport Mercury*, Newport, RI (*NM*); *New York Daily Tribune*, New York City, NY (*NYDT*); *New York Herald*, New York City, NY (*NYH*); *New York Times*, New York City, NY (*NYT*); *New York World*, New York City, NY (*NYW*); *North America and United States Gazette*, Philadelphia, PA (*NAUSG*); *Oxford Democrat*, Paris, ME (*OD*); *Pennsylvania Daily Telegraph*, Philadelphia, PA (*PDT*); *Philadelphia Inquirer*, Philadelphia, PA (*PI*); *Pittsburgh Daily Gazette*, Pittsburgh, PA (*PDG*); *Portland Press Herald*, Portland, ME (*PPH*); *Providence Daily Journal*, Providence, RI (*PDJ*); *Providence Daily Post*, Providence, RI (*PDP*); *Providence Evening Press*, Providence, RI (*PEP*); *St. Albans Daily Messenger*, St. Albans, VT (*SADM*); *Syracuse Daily Courier and Union*, Syracuse, NY (*SDCU*); *The Cecil Whig*, Elkton, MD (*TCW*); *The Columbia Spy*, Columbia, PA (*TCS*); *The Evening World*, New York, NY (*TEW*); *The Union and Journal*, Biddeford, ME (*TUJ*); *Vermont Chronicle*, Windsor, VT (*VC*); *Vermont Phoenix*, Brattleboro, VT (*VP*); *Walton's Daily Journal*, Montpelier, VT (*WDJ*).

PLATE COMMENTARIES

A: NEW YORK

(1) Sergeant, 13th New York Infantry, 1861

The state-issue jacket (fastened by eight Staff buttons bearing the state "Military Seal"; see **1a**) and plain trousers worn by this NCO were made of rusty-gray cloth, trimmed with mid-blue, which deteriorated very quickly. Headgear is a dark-blue high-crowned Pattern-1858 forage cap with black leather visor and chinstrap, and small brass buttons bearing the New York coat of arms and brass letters "NYV" (New York Volunteers) fixed to its top. Footwear consists of "Jefferson" boots. He is taking aim with a Model 1841 "Mississippi" rifle with leather sling. Accouterments include a Pattern 1857 cartridge box with Pattern 1858 oval "US" plate on the outer flap, carried on a shoulder belt bearing a Pattern 1826 round "eagle" plate. A Pattern 1839 oval "US" plate fastens his waist belt on which is carried a Pattern 1855 Allegheny Arsenal percussion-cap pouch with "shield"-shaped outer flap, and a Pattern 1855 socket bayonet in scabbard. Suspended from his right shoulder via a white cotton sling is a New York depot-pattern canteen with a woolen cover and soldier's initials "J.B.O." stenciled on one side. Also carried is a white cotton haversack filled with provisions.

(2) Private, 7th New York Cavalry, 1863

Loading a Sharps New Model 1859 carbine, this private wears a Pattern 1854 mounted service jacket with a single row of 12 small "General Service" buttons at the front and two on each cuff. The lower-than-regulation standing collar is edged with green wool trim and has two green false buttonholes either side. It also has green-trimmed back-seams, cuffs, edging, and rear bolsters. The top of his Pattern 1858 forage cap has a dragoon/cavalry brass "crossed sabers" insignia attached, with the regimental number "1" above and the letters "M" (Mounted) and "R" (Rifles) either side. Two small "General Service" buttons secure the chinstrap. His sky-blue kersey wool mounted service trousers have a reinforced seat and inner leg. Footwear consists

Made by the Paris-based military outfitter Alexis Godillot, this Pattern 1860 black leather shako was worn for full dress by the 73d New York Infantry. (Military & Historical Image Bank CWc28ds)

of ankle, or half-boots, worn in regulation-fashion under the trousers. He is also armed with a Colt Model 1860 Army Revolver and Model 1860 light-cavalry saber with brass-wound leather grip, brass pommel, and brass guard. His waist belt is fastened with a Pattern 1851 "eagle" plate and accouterments include a carbine cartridge box and sling.

(3) Private, 140th New York Infantry, 1864

This Zouave wears the uniform received by his regiment on January 7, 1864. For full dress, his fez has a turban wrapped around it. His jacket with imitation vest attached is bound with red trim and has a red *tombeau* cut from one piece of cloth plus three red cloth-covered buttons added to its top end to create the semblance of a trefoil. A silvered metal badge (**3a**) denoting V Corps, Army of the Potomac, is pinned to his chest. His vest has nine small brass ball buttons along its right edge. His full pantaloons are tucked into yellow leather *jambières* (gaiters) worn over white canvas gaiters. A dark-blue worsted sash bound with red trim is wrapped around his waist. He is armed with a Springfield Model 1842 rifled musket with fixed bayonet. Accouterments include a Pattern 1864 cartridge box with embossed "US" in oval on the outer flap; a waist belt with Pattern 1839 oval "US" plate; and a New York depot-pattern canteen plus waterproofed haversack.

B: PENNSYLVANIA

(1) Private, 5th Regiment, Pennsylvania Reserve Corps, 1861

Armed with a Springfield Model 1842 rifled musket, this soldier holds an example of Army rations consisting of a cracker or biscuit known as hardtack. He wears the light-blue jacket and trousers issued as full dress to the Pennsylvania Reserve Corps during July 1861. Based on that issued to regular Army mounted service troops since 1854, the jacket has a single row of 12 small "General Service" buttons at the front. The collar, cuffs, and non-regulation shoulder straps are plain. Headgear consists of a Pattern 1858 forage cap. His trousers are tucked into tall drab canvas leggings, each fastened by small buttons. Accouterments include a Pattern 1861 cartridge box suspended from a shoulder belt with Pattern 1826 "eagle" plate, Pattern 1850 cap pouch, Pattern 1858 smooth-sided canteen with brown leather strap, and white cotton haversack.

(2) Private, Anderson Body Guard, or Anderson Troop, 1862

Headgear worn by this private consists of a Pascal Havelock stiffened felt cap with flat-black leather visor at front, and felt flaps from the main body of the cap, which was worn folded down or fastened up on to the visor via metal studs and keepers. The letters "RA" embroidered on a circular badge over a dragoon/cavalry metal "crossed sabers" insignia (**2a**) are the initials of Brigadier General Robert Anderson, hero of the defense of Fort Sumter in April 1861, for whom this unit was named. His state-issue Pattern 1854 mounted service jacket is trimmed with red cord and has more non-regulation trim either side of the 12 "General Service" buttons and around the cuffs. Brass scales adorn his shoulders. He wears ankle, or half, boots under his mounted service trousers. Standing at "Present Saber," he is armed with a Model 1860 light-cavalry saber, holstered Colt Model 1861 New Pattern Navy Revolver, and Sharps Model 1859 carbine attached to a carbine sling. Other accouterments attached to his waist belt include carbine and pistol cartridge boxes and a percussion-cap pouch.

(3) Private, Co. A, 76th Pennsylvania Volunteer Infantry (Keystone Zouaves), 1861

In the first uniform issued to the 76th Pennsylvania Volunteer Infantry, this Zouave wears a Pattern 1861 forage cap with sky-blue band and small brass company letter "A" at front. His rather plain jacket has broad, sky-blue facings around the edges and cuffs. Underneath this is a dark-blue shirt with four small metal buttons. A black silk necktie is worn directly around his neck. His plain sky-blue trousers are tucked into off-white colored canvas leggings. He is loading an Enfield Pattern 1853 rifled musket and his accouterments consist of a waist belt with Pattern 1850 Militia "eagle" panel plate on which is carried a bayonet in scabbard, Pattern 1850 percussion-cap pouch, Pattern 1861 cartridge box, and black-painted haversack.

C: MASSACHUSETTS

(1) First Sergeant, 1st Massachusetts Infantry, 1861

Holding his musket at "Secure Arms" to shelter it from the rain, this NCO wears the gray uniform and headgear supplied to his regiment via the Committee on Military Supplies, of Boston, in May 1861. His forage cap has a red band and top, and the metal letters "CLI" (Chadwick Light Infantry) at front. His nine-button chasseur-pattern jacket has red trim on the collar, edges of the shoulder straps, around the cuffs and jacket edges. Rank is indicated by the lozenge above three chevrons on each upper sleeve. A Union cockade (**1a**) is attached to his chest. His dismounted-pattern trousers have a 1½in.-wide red stripe. Also commensurate with his rank, a red worsted sash with worsted bullion fringe ends is worn under his waist belt. Footwear consists of black leather "Jefferson" bootees. He is armed with a Springfield Model 1855 rifled musket with brown leather sling, and a sergeant's sword in scabbard. Accouterments consist of an NCO waist belt with Pattern 1851 "eagle" plate; bayonet in scabbard; Pattern 1861 cartridge box attached to a shoulder belt with Pattern 1826 "eagle" plate; Pattern 1855 Allegheny Arsenal percussion-cap pouch with "shield"-shaped front; Pattern 1858 Philadelphia Depot canteen with jean cloth cover; and black-painted haversack.

(2) Private, Co. K, 19th Massachusetts Infantry, 1863

Drinking from a patent filter canteen with brown wool cover, this Zouave wears a turned-up dark-blue fez with a light-blue worsted tassel. His jacket is trimmed with ball buttons and edged with broad mid-blue lace, and has non-traditional *tombeaux* consisting of "S"-shaped lace terminating in a loop at each end. His cuffs have a geometric pattern formed by folding the lace to form a large diamond with smaller diamonds at each corner. Under this is worn a separate dark-blue vest. Wide sky-blue trousers are tucked into off-white canvas leggings. A plain mid-blue worsted sash with fringed ends is worn under a waist belt with an oval "US" plate, bayonet frog, percussion-cap pouch, and Pattern 1861 cartridge box attached. He holds an Enfield Pattern 1853 rifled musket.

(3) Private, 1st Company, Mounted Rifle Rangers, Massachusetts Volunteers, 1862

The Havelock hat with visor and brim at the back and sides worn by this soldier was patented by Jonathan F. Whipple and made by the Seamless Clothing Manufacturing Company of New York City. Attached to its front are the small brass letters "MRR" (Mounted Rifle Rangers). His state-issue Pattern 1854 mounted service jacket has a low-cut non-regulation collar and green "riflemen" branch-of-service trim. Brass scales adorn his

The uniforms worn by these enlisted men of the City Guard, of Pittsburgh, who enlisted as Co. K, 12th Pennsylvania Volunteer Infantry, are examples of the shoddy clothing worn by some of the first Pennsylvania volunteers in April–May 1861. Standing at far right, Private Samuel B.M. Young would return to service as a commissioned captain of the 4th Pennsylvania Cavalry and rose to the rank of brigadier general by 1865. After the Civil War he became first president of the Army War College at Carlisle, Pennsylvania, and first chief of staff of the US Army. (USAHEC, S.B.M. Young collection)

shoulders. He has sky-blue kersey wool mounted service trousers, and footwear consists of ankle boots with spurs attached. He carries a Sharps New Model 1859 carbine, and is also armed with a holstered Colt Model 1860 Army Revolver and Model 1840 saber with brass-wound leather grip. Accouterments include a cavalry sword belt with Pattern 1851 "eagle" plate, percussion-cap pouch, and carbine sling. Cartridge boxes for carbine and revolver were carried on the rear of his sword belt.

D: NEW JERSEY

(1) Corporal, 9th New Jersey Infantry, 1862

Armed with a Springfield Model 1861 rifled musket, this corporal wears a state-issue Pattern 1851 frock coat with green branch-of-service trim on the collar and cuffs, and nine large "General Service" buttons down the front and two small buttons of the same pattern on each cuff. His sky-blue trousers have ½in.-wide green seam stripes. Headwear consists of a Pattern 1858 hat with green worsted cord, Pattern 1858 brass "eagle" plate, single black ostrich feather plume, and brass horn insignia at front. Accouterments are composed of a Pattern 1861 cartridge box with Pattern 1839 oval "US" plate on the outer flap suspended from a shoulder belt with Pattern 1826 "eagle" plate; waist belt with Pattern 1839 oval "US" plate supporting a Pattern 1850 percussion-cap pouch and frog and bayonet in scabbard; Pattern 1858 canteen suspended from white cloth strap; and black-painted canvas haversack.

(2) Private, 35th New Jersey Infantry, 1864

Standing at "Parade Rest," this Zouave private wears a "Hawkins' Zouave"-pattern uniform acquired from the US Clothing Department in New York City. This consists of a dark-blue wool felt fez with tape binding on the bottom edge and a yellow wool tassel. His jacket is trimmed in maroon worsted wool braid and cord piping with matching braid and maroon wool *tombeaux* with orange centers. The cuffs are closed with hooks and eyes. Worn under the jacket is a dark-blue wool vest trimmed with maroon braid with inset welted pockets.

His matching semi-Zouave trousers have 1in.-wide welts on the outer seams. Off-white canvas leggings with a 1in.-wide band of leather at the top are laced rather than buttoned. He is armed with a Springfield Model 1864 rifled musket and accouterments consist of a Pattern 1864 cartridge box with impressed oval "US" plate, carried on a shoulder belt, under the jacket, with Pattern 1826 "eagle" plate; and a waist belt with Pattern 1839 oval "US" plate on which is carried a Pattern 1850 percussion-cap pouch, plus frog with bayonet in scabbard. He carries a Pattern 1858 Philadelphia Depot canteen with jean cloth cover and cloth strap, and a black-painted haversack.

(3) Private, 3d New Jersey Cavalry (The Butterflies), 1864
Designed to encourage recruitment, this soldier's flamboyant uniform consists of a tall forage cap with small sloping black patent-leather visor, and a yellow metal wreath with the regimental number "3" inset, also shown as a detail (3a). His jacket has three rows of small ball buttons connected by double strands of yellow chest braid, plus small loops in between the buttons and large connecting end loops. The collar is edged with yellow braid and the red patch at front is embellished with two small yellow braid blind buttonholes terminating in smaller ball buttons. A trefoil of double braid embellishes the cuffs. Over this is worn a hooded talma of mid-blue trimmed with yellow with red lining, which has cloth tab fastenings. His sky-blue kersey wool Pattern 1861 mounted service trousers have 2in.-wide yellow welts on the outer seams. Over the trousers are worn knee-high black leather top-boots. He carries a Model 1860 Spencer Carbine, and is also armed with a Remington revolver and Model 1860 light-cavalry saber. Accouterments include pistol and carbine cartridge boxes and percussion-cap pouch. Horse equipment includes a Pattern 1859 saddle, dragoon blanket with orange border, plus bridle and halter with Pattern 1859 cavalry curb bit.

E: NEW HAMPSHIRE
(1) Corporal, Co. F, 3d New Hampshire Infantry, 1861
The brown cloth Havelock hat worn by this corporal was made by hatters Purinton & Ham, of Dover, New Hampshire, and consists of a cloth-covered visor and back flap. The company letter "F" is pinned at its front. Patterned on that prescribed for the US Army in 1851, his state-issue frock coat has a plain collar and sky-blue trim on its cuffs, with rank chevrons of the same color. All buttons are "General Service" pattern. Matching trousers have a ½in.-wide sky-blue welt on the outer seams. He is armed with an Enfield Pattern 1853 rifled musket, and holds a privately purchased Bowie knife with patriotic German silver fittings. His accouterments include a waist belt with Pattern 1839 oval "US" plate, Pattern 1850 percussion-cap pouch, and frog with bayonet in scabbard. His Pattern 1861 cartridge box is suspended from a shoulder belt with Pattern 1826 "eagle" plate attached. A white cotton haversack with three-button flap and a Pattern 1858 canteen with gray wool cover are carried on his left hip.

(2) Private, Co. G, 6th New Hampshire Infantry, 1862
Headgear worn by this private consists of a second-pattern Havelock cap made by Purinton & Ham. Shaped like an orthodox forage cap, it has a black leather visor and chinstrap at front, and a larger black leather visor around the sides and rear. A small company letter "G" is attached to its front. His state-issue dark-blue frock coat is of non-regulation pattern made by clothiers Lincoln and Shaw, of Concord, New Hampshire. Of poor-quality cloth, it has a plain collar and cuffs, and sky-blue trim around its shoulder straps. His

sky-blue kersey trousers are plain. He holds an Austrian Lorenz Modell 1854 Type I rifled musket with leather sling. Slung on his back is a Joseph Short patent knapsack of heavy black enameled canvas with brown leather straps, with a blanket roll attached. Other accouterments include a Pattern 1861 cartridge box with an oval "US" plate, a black-painted haversack, and a Pattern 1858 canteen with wool cover stenciled with "6 N H" (2a).

(3) Musician, Co. A, 15th New Hampshire Infantry, 1863
Playing a wooden fife with pewter mouthpiece, this musician wears a commercial-grade forage cap, affixed to the top of which is his company letter above a militia-pattern infantry horn with the regimental number "15" set inside its loop, and the letters "NHV" (New Hampshire Volunteers) arced below (see 3a). His regulation frock coat has musician's sky-blue "herringbone" braid across the chest and matching trim around the collar and cuffs. He wears plain sky-blue kersey wool trousers. A Model 1840 Musician's sword is carried in a leather frog on his waist belt, which is fastened by a Pattern 1839 oval "US" plate. Other accouterments include a bayonet in scabbard and percussion-cap pouch.

F: RHODE ISLAND
(1) Musician, 2d Rhode Island Infantry, 1861
Beating a snare drum, this musician wears a plain dark-blue chasseur-pattern forage cap with black leather visor, and a chinstrap with small "General Service" buttons at each end. His state-issue plain dark-blue Burnside-pattern blouse has three small buttons on its placket front and one on each gathered cuff, plus a pocket on the chest. His trousers are plain gray kersey. He is armed with a Colt Model 1851 Navy Revolver in an open holster. His waist belt is fastened with a Pattern 1839 oval "US" plate and carries a Pattern 1855 Allegheny Arsenal cap pouch with "shield" front, and a pistol cartridge box. A white webbing sling supports his instrument.

(2) Private, 1st Rhode Island Light Artillery, 1862
This private wears a Pattern 1861 forage cap with black glazed waterproof cover. Based on the 1854 mounted service pattern, his state-issue jacket has nine large buttons bearing the state coat of arms (see 2a) at front and two small buttons of the same type on each cuff. Its collar has scarlet trim on the bottom seam only, and regulation inverted-"V" shape on each cuff. His plain sky-blue kersey trousers are of the mounted service pattern with a reinforced seat and inner leg. Over these are black leather cavalry boots with spurs attached. His brown leather enlisted mounted service belt with two-piece Pattern 1834 "US" plate has hangers attached to accommodate his Model 1840 light-artillery saber in a metal scabbard. He also carries a holstered Colt Navy Revolver, percussion-cap pouch, and pistol cartridge box on his belt.

(3) Private, Co. H, 10th Rhode Island Infantry, 1861
The Zouave wears the original uniform acquired by his unit in July 1861. His red fez has a blue tassel, and his slate-blue jacket is trimmed with orange lace and has orange trefoil and *tombeau* lace on each side of the chest. Five small ball buttons are sewn along the cuff under seam. A pale-blue worsted sash is wrapped around his waist. Tucked into off-white canvas gaiters, his scarlet pantaloons have a double welt of yellow lace on the outer seams. He is armed with a Springfield Model 1835/40 musket converted from flintlock to percussion. His waist belt has a plain rectangular plate, and has attached a bayonet in scabbard, percussion-cap pouch, and Pattern 1861 cartridge box.

G: CONNECTICUT, VERMONT, AND MAINE

(1) Corporal, 1st Connecticut Heavy Artillery, 1862

On guard duty standing at "Order Arms," this corporal wears a Pattern 1861 forage cap with a stamped-brass infantry horn affixed to its top, and a small "General Staff" button either end of the chinstrap. His Pattern 1851 frock coat has scarlet chevrons on each sleeve and is trimmed with scarlet cord around the collar and cuffs. It has nine large gilt Connecticut state buttons down its front (see **1a**), two at waist level at the back, and two smaller buttons of the same pattern on each cuff. Brass shoulder scales and white gloves are in keeping with full dress. His sky-blue kersey wool trousers have a ½in.-wide scarlet welt on the outer seams. He is armed with a Springfield Model 1842 rifled musket. Accouterments include a Pattern 1861 cartridge box suspended from a shoulder belt with Pattern 1826 "eagle" plate attached. His waist belt has a Pattern 1839 oval "US" plate, and carries a Pattern 1850 percussion-cap pouch and socket bayonet in scabbard.

(2) Private, Co. H, 2d Vermont Infantry, 1861

Ramming a ball into an Enfield Pattern 1853 rifled musket, this private wears a gray chasseur-pattern forage cap with black leather chinstrap and a small "state seal" button at each end, and a small metal company letter "H" at front. His state-issue gray frock coat is patterned after Federal regulations but has light-blue trim around collar and shoulder straps. This has nine large state coat of arms buttons at front, two smaller buttons of the same pattern on the under seam of each cuff, and one on each shoulder strap (see **2a**). A pressed-metal "Mounted Riflemen" cap insignia is pinned on the left breast, which may indicate that he belonged to a flank company. His accouterments include a Pattern 1861 cartridge box on a shoulder belt with Pattern 1826 "eagle" plate. On his waist belt with Pattern 1839 oval "US" plate is a percussion-cap pouch and bayonet in scabbard. A black-painted haversack and Pattern 1858 canteen are carried on his left hip.

(3) Farrier, 1st Maine Cavalry, 1864

Examining a bamboo horse-measuring stick, this farrier wears a Pattern 1858 cavalry "Hardee" hat with yellow wool hat cord, black ostrich feather plume, Pattern 1858 brass "eagle" plate pinning up the brim on right, and Pattern 1858 "crossed sabers" insignia at front. Based on the 1854 mounted service pattern, his state-issue jacket has a low collar edged with yellow lace, with a single yellow blind buttonhole inset. Non-regulation yellow lace runs down either side of the 12 "General Service" buttons at front. Cuffs are also trimmed yellow with two small "General Service" buttons on the under seam. A yellow wool "Farrier" insignia is sewn on his left sleeve. Dragoon-pattern boots are worn over his sky-blue mounted service trousers with 1½in.-wide yellow welts on the outer seams. He is armed with a Model 1860 light-cavalry saber, Burnside Fourth Model carbine, and Colt Model 1860 Army Revolver. Accouterments consist of a sword belt with Pattern 1851 "eagle" plate, holster, percussion-cap pouch, cartridge boxes for carbine and revolver, and carbine shoulder strap.

H: DELAWARE, MARYLAND, AND DISTRICT OF COLUMBIA

(1) First Sergeant, 1st Battalion Delaware Cavalry, 1863

The state-issue mid-blue mounted service jacket worn by this cavalry NCO has 12 small "General Service" buttons at the front, and solid branch-of-service yellow facing on the collar and plain cuffs. The lozenge and chevrons on his sleeves are also in branch-of-service color. A red worsted sash denoting rank is wrapped around his waist. Headwear consists of a plain

Worn by Major Walter W. Cochrane, 3d Vermont Infantry, this high-crown chasseur cap bears the maker's mark "Bent & Bush/Corner of/Court & Washington St./Boston" on the leather covering on the underside of the crown. Aged 40, Cochrane received his major's commission in the 3d Vermont Infantry on July 12, 1861, but resigned on August 6 due to disability caused by a severe attack of fever. (Dr. Michael R. Cunningham collection)

dark-blue Pattern 1858 forage cap with a black leather chinstrap and small "General Service" button at each end. His buckskin gauntlets are privately purchased. Tall boots are worn under his sky-blue kersey mounted service trousers, which have 1½in.-wide yellow welts on the outer seams. Arms consist of a Model 1860 light-cavalry saber in a metal scabbard and Colt Model 1860 Army Revolver in holster. Accouterments include a cavalry waist belt with Pattern 1851 "eagle" plate, plus cap pouch and pistol cartridge box.

(2) Private, Co. C, 1st Regiment Potomac Home Brigade, Maryland Cavalry, 1861

Firing his Sharps New Model 1859 carbine, this private wears a plain Pattern 1858 forage cap, and state-issue dark-blue sack coat with eight-button front, a single small button on each shoulder strap, plain cuffs, and yellow trim around the low collar and shoulder straps. Tall dragoon boots are worn over his sky-blue kersey trousers, which are of the mounted service pattern. He is also armed with a holstered Colt Model 1860 Army Revolver. His waist belt has a Pattern 1851 "eagle" plate, and other accouterments include a Watervliet Arsenal percussion-cap pouch and carbine cartridge box.

(3) Corporal, 1st Regiment, District of Columbia Cavalry, 1864

Carrying a McClellan saddle (**3a** shows the shield on the pommel), this cavalry corporal wears a black brimmed felt hat with brasses reading "1" over "DC" attached indicating unit designation. His regulation Pattern 1854 mounted service jacket with 12 "General Service" buttons at the front, and two of the same pattern on the cuffs, is trimmed on the collar, cuffs, and edges in yellow cord and lace. Yellow worsted corporal's chevrons are sewn on his upper sleeves. His sky-blue trousers have ½in.-wide yellow welts on the outer seams and are tucked into dragoon-pattern boots. Arms consist of a Model 1860 light-cavalry saber, Colt Model 1851 Navy Revolver, and Henry rifle slung over his right shoulder via a leather sling attached to rings on the left side of barrel and butt. Accouterments include a black leather sword-hanger strap, waist belt with Pattern 1851 plate, and percussion-cap pouch, plus pistol and cartridge boxes.

INDEX

References to illustration captions are shown in **bold**. Plates are shown with page and caption locators in brackets.